D1376624

Chico's Promise

A Superhero, Lives Saved and a Promise Made!

Mike Monahan

ISBN 978-1-7366853-0-3

Published by:
ThinkMonahan, LLC
414 Main Street
Milford, Ohio 45150

Email: mikemonahan@thinkmonahan.com

Library of Congress Control Number: 2021903865

Author: Mike Monahan

Cover Art of Chico: Alicia Riley

Book Layout and Design: Craig Ramsdell, Ramsdell Design

Printed and bound in The United States of America by:
CJK Print Possibilities

Dedication

To Chico, U.S. Army, tattoo # 66A9,
46th Scout Dog Platoon,

Tay Ninh Vietnam, and to all the
dogs that served in Vietnam

saving tens of thousands of lives. Especially the 4300+ that
were left behind or euthanized after serving our country.

Chico was my partner walking point
(first in line leading patrols)
in the Vietnam War in 1969-1970.

Mike Monahan
Pointman1

chico #66A9
Superhero

Contents

Foreword
By Thane Maynard

When Jane Goodall began her seminal research into wild chimpanzee behavior 60 years ago, she rocked the world of science by showing that individual animals have varying personalities, moods, and desires. Before that, ethologists and behaviorists looked at all animals as organisms with the very same traits. When Jane began her research, it was not considered "scientific" to give animals names — numbers were more appropriate.

There is a famous story of the first time Jane presented her research findings at The Royal Society in London — the very chamber where Newton presented the laws of gravity in the 1680s and Darwin the theory of natural selection in the 1850s. She was a young woman in her 20s who had not yet attended university, and the world-leading experts in attendance tried to throw her off the stage, saying that she didn't know what she was doing and she had never even been to college. But of course Jane stood her ground and said that while she was not as learned as those male professors, she did have a wonderful teacher when she was a girl, who taught her about animal behavior.

Rusty the farm dog was Jane's most constant and beloved companion during her youth on a farm near Bournemouth, England. And Rusty showed her every day about the different moods and curiosities animals can exhibit. So, it was no surprise at all to Jane years later that her beloved chimpanzees were much the same. And to this day it is fair to say that Jane

Goodall loves dogs even more than she loves chimpanzees, or even most people!

There is a reason for our great love for dogs. Descended from wolves, dogs were our companions around the campfire and the hunt even before there were modern humans. In fact, our affection for dogs goes so deep that an old friend who is a veterinarian tells me that most of his customers loved their dogs way more than they did their spouses! I am sure it has something to do with unconditional loyalty.

Which gets us to the story of Chico.

Mike Monahan is disarming. Just ask anyone who knows him.

He is not disarming because of charm or spin, like some people. He disarms you with his honesty, frankness, and willingness to say, not just what he is thinking, but what you are thinking.

I have known Mike Monahan for decades and I am proud to say that this book, *Chico's Promise*, is his best. That, of course, is because he is not giving you his opinion, he is sharing the real history of how it all went down over 50 years ago. And the best part is that you cannot help but love and admire Chico, who also tells it like it is.

This is a story of unconditional loyalty taken all the way to the grave.

Introduction

by Mike Monahan

Imagine for a moment a prominent dog breeder decides to close their business. Now imagine the breeder gathers up hundreds of their dogs and takes them to a dangerous and chaotic location and abandons them. Do you think this is irresponsible behavior on the part of the owner? Do you think it is traumatic for the dogs abandoned and left to fend for themselves? This is not an imaginary story; it is what the U.S. Government did to over 4300 War Dogs. These hero dogs were on the front line of the Vietnam War. When the war ended, and the decision was made to pull out the remaining U.S. troops, the military War Dogs were left behind.

This is Chico's story, one of the hero dogs of the Vietnam War. Chico was a scout dog, a decorated hero who was needlessly put down in the prime of his life. I don't consider this book to be a war story — it is a love story that needs to be shared about a Superhero. I was Chico's partner and handler in Vietnam in 1969. I wrote this book out of gratitude for his saving my life and wrote it in his voice, imagining what he might have said if he could speak in words. The following events are my way to describe my reasons for writing this book for Chico before I go to my grave. I hope the world will love Chico as much as I love him.

Over the past 50 years I have rescued a few dogs from the SPCA and other shelters. One of my favorites was a dog my wife, Nancy, and I saw while on a seminar retreat in Loveland, Ohio. This poor dog looked like he had been abused, and he was in failing health. When the seminar ended, we returned home and I thought the dog was just a memory, but then a week later Nancy told me we had to go get him because it turned out that someone else who had rescued him couldn't keep him. We picked him up and thought he would only live a short time. The vet told us he was an English setter and explained what to do to remedy his ailments. We named him Benny, and to my amazement he rebounded and was a member of our family for the next ten years.

Benny changed my heart. Even though I had several dogs before him, he showed me that I had a wound in my heart that had never healed. At age 20 I was sent to fight in the Vietnam War. My job was to walk point, as first man on patrol, with my scout dog Chico. I was blessed and made it out alive, but when it was time to come home, I had to leave Chico behind. Chico had saved my life several times and he saved many other soldiers' lives, too.

I was excited to return home, but I had to abandon Chico because the Army said he had to stay. I blamed the Army, but the sadness and guilt continued to fester inside me over the years and showed up adversely in many of my relationships and reactions to life.

The effects of war led to some destructive behavior on my part, like too much drinking and a marriage ending in divorce. I was angry and fighting against any authority trying to tell me what to do, like leaving Chico behind. The feelings of abandoning Chico were much deeper than I had realized and played out in my behavior. I wasn't kind to many of my dogs after I returned home; I was more interested in trying to control them than love them. Then Benny appeared and my heart began to heal.

I was a single dad raising four children, and I decided to remarry. My new wife, Nancy, had a young son, and so we faced the challenges of being newly married and having a blended family. I changed careers, and quit drinking and smoking, and life was getting better. That's when Benny entered the picture and touched me in much the same way that Chico had touched me in Vietnam, and in retrospect, I realized that I was trying to rescue myself from my guilt by rescuing dogs from shelters. But I discovered that saving dogs couldn't fill the hole I had in my heart for Chico if I didn't love myself. If I didn't do that, I couldn't help but treat everyone and everything, including my dogs, with disrespect.

Benny began the healing process so I could move forward, not move on! After Benny passed, I bought an English setter puppy as a companion for Nancy right before she was scheduled for brain surgery, and Nancy named her Belle. Belle filled my heart with more love and was with us for twelve years before passing. Her death was difficult for both Nancy and me, so we waited a while before considering another dog. After six months we decided to rescue another English setter, and we traveled from our home in Florida to Oklahoma to pick up our new puppy. Doogie has been with us two years now and is a permanent member of the family.

With my heart full I could finally write my love story about Chico, who has lived in my heart and mind for fifty years. In the beginning it was sadness, but today it is love. Now is the time for the world to hear from my Superhero as I imagine he might tell his story. My dream is that millions of people will read Chico's story, fall in love with him, become inspired, and join forces to improve the treatment of dogs by eliminating abuse and abandonment. If Chico were alive today, I know he would make that promise.

Early Memories

Eat, Sleep, and Play

Hi, I'm Chico. As they say, "You don't know what you don't know." At the very beginning of my life I felt warm, secure, and loved — part of a massive ball of fur and paws in a mob of excited and playful chaos. I felt super special alongside my nine siblings, and mom seemed to do nothing more than try to protect her body parts from being suckled off her chest.

She was one fine looking bitch, and as I recall, Lois said mom was a Silver German Shepherd, but I'm just taking Lois's word for it. I found the whole dog breed topic was brought up more as we got older so Lois could drive up the price on the sale of us pups. Lois swore my dad was a collie, but you'll never convince me that he sired me and the rest of the pack. Lois may not have been around at the moment of conception, nor was I, but when I was a week old I can remember a heated argument Lois had with a neighbor telling him to "Keep your damn husky off my property," which leads to my suspicion as to who's my real dad. In the end only Mom can say, and she's not talking.

My being part husky is only speculation, but it's also instinct based on my traits. Shepherds, as most people know, make good guard dogs. We are protectors. If you crossbreed us with a collie you are just crossing out innate behaviors, because collies like to herd things into a group, like herding sheep to a specific area. Or they want to feel like they belong to a certain group of people, thus creating confusion for either guarding against as opposed to gathering up. Just follow my reasoning for a moment. I think my dad was the neighbor's husky. While Huskies, on the other hand, look like cute balls of fur as pups but are known to be very aggressive sometimes as they mature. I felt like a loner even among the puppy pack and have always tended to be somewhat aggressive, especially when someone invades my space. I'm not a hang-out-with-people kind of dog. I'm loyal to the right person if I can trust them, but the rest of the world better stay out of my space. And with that deduction I've eliminated the theory of a collie being my dad.

Dinner time was what you could call tit for tat. When there are ten mouths to feed and you only have eight teats, things can get rather pushy. I decided that I was going to be on the tit side eating at the head of the breast table, not the tat side being left out and becoming the runt of the litter. Mom always seemed to figure out a way for everyone to get a turn on a teat at the table, but for the life of me, I don't know how she did it while keeping herself intact.

My assertiveness showed from the beginning. I was a dog on a mission when it came to mealtime — always on point and first dog on a teat, determined not to be sucking hind tit here or anywhere else in my life. While several members of my litter were jockeying in and out of the litter trying to find a place, I was already half finished with my meal. I loved sitting at the head of the table because beyond having a full belly, I received extra attention from mom. She was so soft and gentle, as I suckled, and would always take the time to lick my face and nuzzle my ears with her nose. I felt safe and loved with her breathing in my ear. She didn't actually talk to me, I guess, but with each breath in my ear I could imagine her saying, "I love you, little boy." Till the day I die I will remember her distinct scent. I have never smelled that scent any other time. I can't describe it, but I knew she and I were connected. We were one, and yet different from the potpourri of sibling smells. My world was alive and full of adventure. It seemed that my eyes, ears, and nose where exploding in amazement in my new world on the farm. Even at a young age, I knew I had everything I would need to succeed, and I felt like I had a passport to an exciting future.

I don't know if it's true, but I think we must be born knowing who we are and who we are supposed to be in this world. I was born to be a Superhero, although I didn't even know what that meant. And I had three superpowers — my eyes, my ears, and my nose — and they were the ticket to fulfill my purpose. I was always sure that dogs have a purpose.

My sight is best at dusk and dawn, but I found I could see pretty well at night, too, certainly much better than humans. I am also quick to pick up movement caused by the wind or animal movement — I guess that's why humans use dogs for hunting. I do all this without eyeglasses, of course, and thank God, because not having thumbs I could never get a set of contacts in my eyes or glasses on my nose. Of my three superpowers though, I would put my sight last.

Another thing I am eternally grateful for is not having a Basset Hound for a parent. If you ask me, those big floppy ears they have are a complete waste of skin — if they don't pay attention while eating, they can bite an ear. Thank goodness I received the functionally correct set of erect radar-detector ears, and life on the farm was the perfect place to test my hearing skills. There were hundreds of different birds singing unique songs, frogs croaking down by the pond and up in trees. You name it and it was probably in our back pasture making noise. I noticed that I heard certain things humans didn't seem to hear. Sounds for me are so strong, yet humans don't always react to what I have heard until after I heard it. That's one of the reasons why I've concluded I have superpowers that humans don't have, but they can benefit by partnering with me.

Of my three superpowers though, I was sure that my nose was going to be the thing that would set me apart from the rest of the pack. Even at an early age I surprised myself by knowing immediately what Lois had for breakfast in the morning. I quickly surmised that she was a bacon and eggs junkie, and several days a week I could swear she showered in maple syrup. The smell was intense. I could also smell what animals on the farm she had been working with each day because she carried their smell on her clothes. I am sure that humans just don't "get us." On a given afternoon when Lois stopped by, I could smell breakfast, lunch, and who and what she had come in contact with, all because of unique smells. (Let me make this clear, I didn't think my purpose was going to be guessing what people had for breakfast, but I knew my keen sense of smell was going to be a key factor in my future success.). How's that for a superpower?

Back then my days were filled with eating and romping around with the rest of the pack. We had a lot of fun play fighting and chasing each other, and without knowing it, we were determining our ranking order in the pack. Just like being first at eating, I found that I took most things seriously. Even while playing, I was extremely competitive. I wanted to be the best at everything I did, and I gave one hundred percent. I wasn't sure what it meant back then, but I heard Lois telling visitors I was the alpha dog.

All these memories are flooding in on me now as I lie here alone and confused. I find it comforting to think back on my early days on the farm in 1966 with my mom, brothers, and sisters. I loved that time, and I just knew I was going to do something special in my life and maybe become a Superhero. I did all the things that were expected of a Superhero, yet it seemed many of my actions were misunderstood and caused problems later in my life. The consequences I paid then weren't the end of the world — but it looks like my luck just ran out.

Here I am in Vietnam, a decorated war hero, waiting to be put down. The Army calls it being euthanized because they don't want to own the dirty deed, but I know they are about to kill me, and I'm really scared and disappointed. I assumed, being a Superhero, I would go down in a brutal fire fight with the Viet Cong (VC). Or I'd miss seeing a tripwire walking down a trail, and BOOM — I'm blown away! Maybe a sniper's lucky shot would hit the fuel tank and take down the chopper I was on. But did that happen? No! Talk about disappointment. Here I am after being a good soldier and saving hundreds of lives, getting euthanized for being too aggressive. What a slap in the muzzle. What a joke! The Army trained me to become combat infantry, and then they turn around and expect me to be passive. It's very confusing and disappointing.

I've heard humans say that when they die, they want to come back as a dog because they think a dog's life is great. I wonder if the opposite is true: will I come back as a human? If so, I've decided I'll be a high-ranking officer and will be instrumental in changing the Army's attitude toward war dogs.

Enough of what the future may bring. I'm going to use what little time I have remaining to think about the safest and most loving times of my life, like when I was with my mom and siblings, before the challenges of being a Superhero took over my life. As I lie here on this hot metal table, I can remember the scent of my mom. That smell is etched into my brain! God, I miss her, and I hope to see her on my next journey.

My Story

While I'm not what they call purebred, I come from a long line of leaders and am what you might call the pick of the litter. The morning when I first met Dave, I was hanging out with mom and my five brothers and four sisters. (For some reason we didn't have names, they just called us girl or boy. For a while I thought I might have had an identity problem, but I think I've worked through it!) Lois picked me up and wrapped me in a blanket and said to me, "Okay, little boy, it's your lucky day. You're going to meet your new owner. I'm going to surprise my brother Dave with this special little gift."

The moment Dave unwrapped the blanket, I felt so special. He said, "He's beautiful. He has his mother's markings," and he was right. I looked a lot like mom, including that my ears were always at attention assessing what was going on around me. Since I never met my dad, I'm not sure what about me favors him, but I know I must have many of his features. As Dave held me, I remember Lois saying to him, "He's the alpha of the litter, so I couldn't think of a better person to have him than a police officer and my brother." I wasn't sure what "alpha" meant, but I was honored to be the one chosen and to know I was still part of a family.

Soon I was introduced to my new family. Dave was married to Sandy and they had an adorable little girl named Lisa, who soon would be my playmate. Lisa, like me, was a ball of energy. I immediately knew she and I had a future of stirring up a little trouble. And the next thing I knew, I had a name:

Chico. It was a little confusing at first, but quickly I felt like it fit me perfectly.

In the spring of 1968, film coverage of the Vietnam War was all over the evening news, and even though I was a dog, I remember spending a lot of time lying in front of the TV. Every night the evening news seemed to draw a lot of family attention, and I can remember Dave would tell Lisa to go play. He didn't want her to see the coverage of the war and the anti-war protesters on many of the college campuses. Dave knew I could handle tough situations, though, so he let me hang out and watch the news with him and Sandy — just the three of us adults.

Even though I'm fabulous at most things, from watching all the fighting in Vietnam on TV, I instinctively knew serving in that war would be a challenge for me on a few fronts. First, let me say that I'm not afraid of guns, but in tight places the loud sounds of weapon fire are excruciating painful for my ears. Dave was a police officer, so I had spent most of my life around guns and knew how responsible he was. He had enough sense to wear ear protection when he went to the police practice range, and on returning to the house, he always separated the weapon and the ammunition, put them up and out of reach, and locked them away from the family. So, I knew I was in good hands around him with guns.

The favorite part of my day was when Dave returned home safe. I could tell that Sandy worried about him when he was on duty, and I loved to see him come through the front door in his police uniform. I always tried to be first to welcome him home. He was a handsome man and very proud of his work in law enforcement, and he was equally proud of being a good family man. Dave always took the time to kneel down and have a chat with me: "How's my boy? Did you protect everybody while I was at work?" His greeting was always followed by a nice rub behind my ears. Man, I loved that! There is something about a man in uniform I like, but then again, I've overreacted to some men in uniform when I didn't know them. But that's another part of my story.

From my viewpoint, watching the news on TV, war looked a little crazy. For as much as humans declare themselves to be superior beings, they sure didn't seem to have their lives together. They didn't agree with the Vietnamese and so they sent their young people to war. Then if the soldiers were lucky enough to stay alive, when they returned home, the very people who had sent them called them "baby killers." Like I said, a little crazy. Maybe it's time for humans to start paying a little more attention to us canines. Sniffing butts is an effective way to quickly figure out who you like or dislike. If you don't believe me, just go to the park where people walk their dogs and see how quickly we get the whole friend/enemy thing worked out!

The evening news always seemed to focus on stories on the Vietnam War showing soldiers in combat, fighting on the ground and in the air, medics were shown frantically carrying wounded soldiers to helicopters for immediate evacuation to military hospitals. There were scenes of other soldiers loading body bags containing their fallen buddies onto helicopters waiting to fly to base camp to be appropriately processed. Sometimes there were reporters on the same patrol with the troops, capturing photos of soldiers in firefights with the Viet Cong and the North Vietnamese Army (NVA). Some had film coverage of door gunners on the helicopters with M60's blazing, firing hundreds of rounds of bullets as they came in to drop off the soldiers. It was tragic.

As I watched the news, my mind would drift and I'd find myself thinking, "What would I do if I was in Vietnam?" I could only imagine what it would feel like trying to slog through those rice paddies in the monsoon rains or working off a Navy boat down in the Delta. I can swim, but for how long would I be expected to stay afloat? Would they give me ear protection? Those door gunner's M60's would fry my ears. And would I be agile enough to successfully jump on and off the helicopters? I am a pretty good jumper. (As a matter of fact, my jumping skills got me in the biggest trouble of my life with Dave!) When I saw films of some of the terrain, I imagined my greatest difficulty would be trying to navigate through the dense jungle.

Don't get me wrong, I was just trying to understand what I was seeing. The soldiers must depend on each other to stay alive. I understand how it must feel. I'm no different. If somebody threatened anyone I loved, I'd protect them and, if somebody invaded my space or got a little too close to my territory, I've been known to lash out a few times. The way I saw it, Dave's job was to protect everybody in town and my job was to protect the family and our yard. It didn't matter if Dave was at work or at home. In my mind, home territory had been delegated to me to keep it and everyone in it safe. And I took my job seriously. I even got myself into some tight situations because of my need to protect those I cared about. But the good news was I didn't have to worry about the war, even though they kept talking about the draft. I didn't think I was Army material.

I grew fast and everyone said I was a beautiful dog. Dave told everyone how he loved that I didn't shed much. I was happy about that too because I thought I'd look a little strange if I were bald. Now and then I would see my reflection, and I must admit, they were right — a good-looking dog … pick of the litter! I like how my coat is so shiny and not too long or too short, and I think my tan face makes me look distinguished. Like so many great men, I have a beard, and knowing my peers will be checking me out from the rear, I especially love the way my tail arches forward. Like all patriotic Americans flying the flag, when I wag my tail, I look like I'm waving a thousand flags that signal the message "Come smell me." I learned at a young age to show up, go after what I wanted, and always wag my tail to draw attention. Believe me, I know how to get attention!

I think it was instinct or maybe my fine bloodline that gave me clarity about my role in life. I understood my role as protector of the family and the homestead, and I began to understand better what Lois had said about me being an alpha dog. I got in trouble several times with Dave for being a little too aggressive, but in my mind, I was just doing my job. Perception is a funny thing. While I thought I knew my role in the family and took it seriously, Dave seemed to think that I went about it too assertively. That's another strange thing I've observed about humans. They think we are too aggressive when we bite, but they often use their multi-functional tongue to attack and bite others using words! Oh, the double standards I have observed in "The Superior Race" already at my young age: Do as I say, not as I do!

So, figuring out exactly what my role was in the new family was a little confusing, but in time I learned exactly what Dave expected from me. We lived in a cute little house in Tioga, North Dakota. In the early days I liked to collect things from around the neighborhood and bring them home to share with the people I loved. Dave once commented to me that as a police officer he was concerned he might have to arrest me one day for being a thief. My favorite thing was borrowing our neighbor's boots. He would leave them wet and muddy on the porch and, being a concerned citizen and partner to a police officer, I thought I'd help him out. Dave loved to work in the garden, and I don't wear boots, so I would simply leave them for him in our sunny driveway. Dave kept returning the boots to their rightful owner — dry and dirty!

Another thing I loved to do was scout the neighbors' yards in search of interesting laundry. I was quite the expert at pulling things off the clothesline and returning home with my spoils. And then there were those two chickens, just plucked for grilling by our neighbor farmer friend. I was surprised to see him put them on the picnic table before heading back in the house to clean up before grilling, and I couldn't resist such a golden opportunity! When he came out, the chickens were gone and so was I. Dave didn't seem to appreciate my gift of the day. He had to clean the chickens off our driveway before he and Sandy went down the street to the chicken-less barbeque party.

I got into still bigger trouble when two-year-old Lisa and I decided to go on a little adventure. We got up and went out at four in the morning so she could practice riding her trike. Well, this was his daughter, not just chickens, and Dave got pretty upset. So you see, I was a handful right from the beginning. Eventually, Dave was offered a better job as a police officer in Williston, North Dakota, and the whole family moved — except for me. I was left behind. I'm sure it was to protect and scavenge the neighborhood, but that's another story.

The Day My Life Changed

It was right after my second birthday when things came to a boiling point between Dave and me. It was a typical mid-morning on a Saturday, one of those late fall days when the temperature is just right to open the windows and doors and let some fresh air into the house. Dave was out working on fall clean-up in the yard. He loved his gardens and often complained to me about my need to pee on everything in his yard. Humans just don't get it. If their noses worked better, like those of dogs, they would know this is my yard from the scent of my markings, long before they entered the yard. For example, I knew there was a collie a few doors down the street even though I had never been to her yard. I could smell her location, especially when there was a good breeze. But like Dave, the superior race would have to walk down three houses to know that a "cute collie" (my assumption) lived there. My job was to know what was going to happen before it happened. Humans seem to be unaware of so much, and they wait to react — just like with the war in Vietnam.

It was right after lunch when all hell broke loose. Like I said, Dave was out back working in the yard, and I was inside with Lisa. I loved hanging out with Lisa because she was a lot like me. She was three — that's twenty-one in dog years — with an amazing amount of energy. We would run around the house and play fetch with my toys. She tried her best to hide them, but my nose always won in the hide-'n-seek game. She was standing by the front screen door, holding my favorite blue rubber squeak bone. That squeaking noise could drive me into a frenzy, and in that moment, I was primed.

As I stood at attention, waiting for her to throw the bone, a truck stopped right at our front walk, catching my attention. Some guy I'd never seen before in a blue uniform was headed toward the front door. Dave was still out in the back, and this guy had something in his hand. Was it a gun? My only thought was, "Lisa is in danger." I stepped forward, gently nudging Lisa to the side, while waiting on this stranger to get closer. As he reached out, I was thinking he was going to pull the door open and abduct Lisa, but instead he knocked! My protector instincts kicked in, and that was my cue to leap through the screen door and grab his arm for a classic guard-dog take-down.

The perpetrator was yelling at the top of his lungs! Dave rounded the corner of the house to find me hanging on his arm, adorned with a large screen around my neck! All I can remember was Dave screaming, "Chico, NO! NO, Chico!" as I felt his hands around my neck! Why was Dave trying to stop me from protecting Lisa instead of stopping the perpetrator? I was totally confused. Dave was angry, the meterman was panicked and bleeding, and Lisa was in the foyer crying. Things weren't good! How was I supposed to know he was a meterman?

Even though I disagreed with his assessment and reaction, I must admit Dave's police training came into play in this situation. He handled it like a professional. He calmed me down and got me under control. He called for help for the meterman. And he comforted Lisa until she calmed down and stopped crying.

Over the next few days, I could tell something wasn't right. Dave was treating me differently. He wasn't bringing up the meterman situation or throwing it in my face; it was worse. I was getting the cold shoulder, quiet treatment. Eventually, the front screen was replaced. Dave did a great job, and it looked as good as new. I was thinking that we were back to normal now, and we could let bygones be bygones, but as it ended up, it was the day I'll never forget.

Dave put a leash on me and said, "Come on, boy. We're going to take a ride." It wasn't time for my vet check, so I was leery about getting in the truck, but I trusted Dave and I were on the same team. We drove for a short while and I recognized where we were. It was Tioga, the old town where we used to live, but we kept going. Finally, we arrived at a place called Minot Air Force Base and Dave got out and started talking to a guard.

Sign
Me Up

Abandoned

It's all a blur to me from that point on. The next thing I realized was I'm out of Dave's truck and sitting in a cage waiting to be loaded onto a plane. I don't remember getting to say goodbye to Lisa or Sandy, and, as I remember, Dave seemed a little emotional. But all I got was a few pats on the head and "Sorry boy, you'll be fine." Sorry! I thought we were a family! I thought I was doing my job protecting Lisa! I thought we were a team, Dave! But obviously I had missed something along the way because I was being shipped to who knows where — abandoned!

Like I said, most of what happened next is kind of a blur. I was at Minot Air Force Base for a short while and then was flown out to Langley Air Force Base in Hampton, Virginia. Once at Langley, I was put through a series of assessments designed by the military to determine what field of duty I was best suited for. From what I could determine there were five areas of duty: Sentry Dogs, Tracker Dogs, Mine/Booby-Trap Dogs, Tunnel Dogs, and Scout Dogs.

Sentry Dogs were mostly German shepherds assigned to military bases to protect the military compounds. They patrolled inside the perimeter wire to ensure the enemy didn't penetrate the wire defenses. I knew the military criteria for sentry duty was to look for overly aggressive dogs who would attack infiltrators when necessary. I was clear sentry duty wasn't something I wanted, so I acted meek to make sure I wasn't selected. I knew I wanted to make a difference in the field.

After all those nights of watching the evening news with Dave, I knew I was best suited to become an infantry scout dog and a Superhero.

Tracker Dogs were used for finding downed pilots or enemy soldiers. It was obvious I was not in any way suited to be a tracker. There were plenty of Lab mixes that are well-suited to keeping their nose to the ground. Being a Tracker Dog was not my idea of a good use of my spectacular nose. Tunnel Dogs? Again, not my style. Looking for mines and booby traps underground sounded boring to me. However, being a Scout Dog walking point on patrol was definitely the job for my superpowers to shine and save lives. If I played all my cards right, being assertive but not aggressive, holding my head high and letting them see me picking up scents in the wind, I might be selected to be a Scout Dog. Before I knew it, a few others and I were crated up and shipped out to Fort Benning Army Base in Georgia.

Once we landed in Georgia, our shipping cages were loaded onto a military truck called a Deuce and a Half (a 2 ½-ton truck). It was a long hard ride. The metal cage sure wasn't very comfortable. As it bounced around, I felt every crack in the road. Just before dark the truck stopped, and I could hear someone talking to the driver. "Welcome to Fort Benning. Can I help you, private?" "Yes, I am delivering three dogs donated to the canine unit. Here's their paperwork, Kentucky, Gardo, and Chico." I was surprised the driver knew our names.

The sergeant radioed for an escort as he rounded the vehicle to open the tailgate and check the delivery. As the tailgate banged open, I was a little startled, and the next thing I knew I was at red alert attention, growling at the sergeant and the truck driver. The sergeant commented, "He's a beautiful dog but a little aggressive. Whoever gets him is going to have their hands full!" "Yes," the driver said, "that's Chico, and I've heard it's why he's here. His owner said he's a great dog but way too much of a liability because of his aggressiveness. That's why they donated him to the Army."

What bullshit! These two guys didn't know me and they were already spreading rumors. If I could have broken out of that cage, I would have given the two of them something to talk about! So, all those nights I spent watching the news with Dave, smugly thinking I didn't need to worry about getting drafted, I got volunteered. I didn't know someone else could volunteer me, but now I know that Dave, not I, could make the call.

Soon a jeep arrived to escort our truck to the Scout Dog Stake-Out area. As we pulled up, I quickly realized that I was going to be surrounded by my kind of people — dogs, that is. The barking was intense. A couple of Army guys lowered my cage, opened the door, and hooked a leash on my choke chain collar. There had to be over fifty dogs staked out, howling, and barking as I passed by them. Eventually we stopped and they put a leather collar on me, hooked another leash to my new collar, and released the walking leash. I was officially in the Army! I was staked out with the other dogs waiting — on I didn't know what.

When we arrived at the gate, I recalled the driver saying we were in Georgia. It was much warmer there in January than back in North Dakota. I liked it warmer, which was comfortable, but I was sleeping outside instead of in a nice house. Georgia was a much better place to be sent than being shipped to Vietnam in the monsoon season, especially with the recent Tet Offensive they were blasting on the nightly news. Not only did I have to sleep outside in a metal cage, they also didn't give me a TV. How did they expect me to stay up with current events? I think they feared letting us canines become too educated, thinking we might eventually take over the humans. Oh well, it had been a long day, and I needed to get a little sleep.

As it turned out, that's what happened: I got just a <u>little</u> sleep. I lay awake most of the night thinking about how I missed my family and how lonely I felt not knowing what to expect. Guess what I found out? Georgia has pesky sand fleas, and they thought I was their mobile home. I knew from that moment on, military life was going to be a challenge.

Yappers

Daybreak came all too soon. I stretched a little to get my bearings and assess what in the hell was going on. First, I was not too wild about the accommodations — in the middle of the woods, fleas all over the place, confined to a twelve-foot circle, and no bed or TV. It was not your typical Hilton stay!

From what I could see there was a whole cast of characters around me. There were quite a few purebred German shepherds. I had to keep an eye out for them because they could get very temperamental and somewhat aggressive, but obviously not enough bite to have made the cut at Sentry Dog School. I noticed a few mixed Labs. They can be really flaky and easily lose focus. Most Labs would be happy to spend the rest of their lives chasing their own tails. And it looked like us mixed breeds or, as the master race called us, "Mutts" were fairly represented in the group. But a few looked like they came from the same fine canine line as mine.

I only hoped they were going to do something with those yappers, always running their mouths but never acting. When I went through the screen door to save Lisa, I acted by surprising that meterman. I didn't even bark or growl. I'm all about the surprise attack! I wished the yappers would have shut up and somebody would have fed us. I was starving! Food is another one of the things I missed. Sandy could make a mean meal combining a scoop of dry dog food with a medley of nightly table scraps. She knew what I loved to eat!

I can't tell you how long being staked out lasted, but my life was hitting an all-time low. Day after day, chained up with a bunch of yappers, and being fed the worst bland food you can imagine. Instead of a family, I was subjected to listening to the complaining of fifty other dogs, with no opportunity to make a butt check to figure out who I liked or disliked. I only had contact with three people each day, one to drop off my meal, one to replenish my water, and the third with the "clean up" job. Eat, drink, circle, and poop. Really! Was this my destiny for protecting Lisa?

Like I said, I'm not sure how long it lasted. My best guess was a week short of eternity, and then I remembered one night, back in the day on the news, hearing a soldier saying something about the military life was hurry up and wait. I think I got what he was saying. Hallelujah! I overheard two soldiers talking and they were excited. The one told the other that they would soon be off feed detail because a new class of dog handlers had just arrived. I wasn't exactly sure what this news meant for me, but being an optimist, I assumed things were looking up.

That Dog Is Crazy

Soon there was a lot of commotion as the new class of dog handlers arrived. They looked a little nervous. We had new people on feed detail, and they didn't know what to expect. As you may recall, I'm leery of people I don't know, especially if they're in uniform and they cross into my space — like the meterman who sealed my fate and caused me to be here.

Here we go, I thought! Déjà vu all over again! There was a guy in uniform walking up with a bowl in his hand, entering my territory. As he reached in to put down my bowl of food, I was wagging away. He thought it was all good, but he was about to have a rude awakening. I noticed he had on gloves, but I was ready. As he set the bowl down, I nailed him. I had him by the hand and began to drag him in to my area. By the look on his face I could tell he was scared. I was just trying to have a little fun and teach him to respect me and my territory. Eventually I decide to let go, before this dude had a heart attack or shit his pants. In an instant, he jumped back, out of my reach. With a sigh of relief from the pain of my teeth in his hand, he declared, "That dog is crazy!"

I began to understand what my mom's owner had said about me. I didn't like people in my space or telling me what to do. That must be the alpha dog Lois spoke of and Dave called aggressive. So, let me get this straight: humans describe me as an aggressive, alpha male who is crazy, while I think I'm just opinionated and want others to respect my boundaries. Isn't perception a funny thing? I chalked this up as another learning experience and didn't lose any sleep over it. He may have lost some sleep over it, but I will probably never see that guy again! As he walked away, I heard a buddy of his call out, "You okay, Monahan?" As a side note, Monahan did return a few times that week but must have got my message, because he made sure he didn't deliver my meal again. It's good to know that while my tongue doesn't allow me to speak, I communicated clearly with him.

Basic Training

It wasn't very long before we each got a human or, as they called it, a "Scout Dog Handler" to work with us. My handler's name was Lopez. He was a little leery of me in the beginning, and later I found out that Monahan had done a little trash talk about me to Lopez. As it ended up, Monahan's partner, Rommel, was my next-door neighbor in the stake-out area. Rommel was a highly intelligent and sophisticated canine — much too fine a canine to be wasted on the likes of Monahan. I had made up my mind that if I ever had an opportunity I would go after Monahan again, just for kicks.

And so, the training began, but I wasn't sure who was training whom. We started out with what they called basic obedience: heel, sit, stay, and how to follow commands. We canines think humans are trying to control us so they can feel superior and call themselves the "Master Race." Right? I must admit, following orders wasn't my strong suit. I'm smart as any but I didn't like people telling me what to do, and I definitely didn't like somebody jerking me around with a choke chain. I adjusted to Lopez and now and then would growl or snap at him just to let him know I was not a push-over.

After a couple of weeks most of us had the routine down, when to heel and follow all their commands, including some non-verbal signals. Part of the training included a series of "pass-byes" they called a fight line. Lopez and I walked past every dog and their handler at close quarters to break us of fighting with each other. It can be a tough exercise for an alpha dog, if you know what I mean. But I passed the test. I walked past fifty dogs and fifty dogs passed by me without an incident. I didn't want to cause another screen-door scene. The Army might send me to Vietnam or some other godforsaken place worse than Georgia — if it were even possible! I wasn't clear what Scout Dog Training was supposed to accomplish, but then again, much of what these humans did didn't make much sense to me.

I find human behavior interesting. What they called relationship building seems to be nothing more than gaining control. I'm not strictly talking about human-to-dog. It seems to me they work awfully hard to maintain control in their human-to-human relationships. Men especially seem to have that alpha thing going on in most of the things they do! I decided I could navigate through their silly rules while maintaining my canine integrity. Integrity was always of utmost importance to me. If I sacrificed my integrity, I would have abandoned my identity. I refused to compromise my soul's purpose to please a human.

I'm not sure what to expect after my passing from this earth. I saw some specials on "National Geographic" that suggested the possibility of dogs coming back as humans. It sounds like a long shot to me, but if it happens, look out world! You won't be able to shut me up with my new multi-functional tongue!

Time to Scout

The next morning everything changed. They loaded us onto a truck and took us to the scout dog training course. It would take me way too long to describe the chaos of fifty dog teams loading onto trucks, so I will move on to telling my story.

As soon as we got off the truck, one of the platoon sergeants told Lopez to stake me out and come back because he was going to be a decoy. We went to the holding area they had set up for us and Lopez chained me up and then headed back to the trucks. I was kind of confused as to what my role was to be in this training course. I was also a little confused about what the platoon sergeant had said to Lopez. Maybe I misunderstood? Like I said, I spent quite a bit of time in front of the TV at Dave's house and saw my share of nature shows, but the only thing I can recall about decoys involved duck hunting. I couldn't imagine why the Army would be involved in duck hunting unless the enemy was using ducks to carry secret messages like they used carrier pigeons back in the old days.

It dawned on me that I was officially now in the Army. "Hurry Up and Wait" was the order of the day, but patience wasn't my strong suit. I wanted to stay busy but lying around there I found myself rehashing the past and feeling like a victim, and I'll be damned if I wanted to live my life like a victim. After all, I'm a Superhero.

I didn't have to wait too long. Soon Lopez returned and we were off to the training course. There were a few handlers and their dogs waiting to start, so we just relaxed awhile. Eventually the sergeant came over and told Lopez, "Put the scouting harness on your dog and meet me at the starting point." So, Lopez slipped a leather harness over my head and fastened the strap under my chest. Next, he unsnapped the six-foot leash from my choke chain and snapped it on the leather scouting harness, and to my surprise he removed my choke chain completely and stuck it in his pocket. Something big was about to happen and I was jazzed up! I thought I would probably be promoted to "Top Dog!"

What Am I Scouting?

As we waited to get started, I couldn't get over the irony of how humans think when it comes to their relationship with us canines. We are about to start training and all I knew was I am the scout dog. Now Lopez has probably been in hours of training and watched a lot of films to let him know what we would be scouting, but no one has even mentioned what I was supposed to scout. Was I looking for ducks? In the air or on the ground? My great nose can smell any number of things at the same time. For example, I can tell you someone is cooking meat off in the distance and from what direction. I can smell the mild scent of other dogs, probably the scents left behind from the ones who have scouted before me. I can smell so many things at once without even seeing them. And by the way, my eyesight and hearing aren't too shabby either. But my nose is awesome if I do say so myself!

The sergeant announced, "Lopez and Chico, you are up!" Lopez stepped on to the trail and gave me a command — "Scout, boy" — and we were off and moving. I immediately moved from the heel position at his side and took the lead, putting my nose to work. Even though I'd never been around a duck, I was sure I'd be able to pick up the scent based on the many other birds I had been in contact with over the years.

I tried to stay focused on picking up the scent of fowl, but the smell of cooking permeated the air, along with the leftover scents of the dogs and handlers that had traveled the path before us. Some of the handler scents seemed too strong to be residual, so I assumed there were a few handlers in the area. My nose is equipped to continually take in scents and quickly blow it back out to refresh my smelling abilities. I can smell a thousand different things at once with this technique, while at best, Lopez might be smelling only one thing.

We walked for about five minutes or so, and I could feel myself getting charged up with this scouting. Suddenly, out of nowhere, this guy jumped up right in my space, and I was so startled I almost barked! Well, as you probably have already guessed, I was in full-blown, red alert reaction — #1, guy in uniform; #2, I don't know him; #3, he's in my space; and #4, he's running and I'm chasing! Lopez was getting his first lesson in what it's like to handle a canine who has a long line of huskies in his family tree. My guess is he was wondering why they didn't give him a dog sled. I was off in hot pursuit, and the soldier was running as if his life depended on outrunning me. I'm not sure his life depended on it, but surely his ass did! Just as I closed the gap and was prepared to take him down, I heard him yell, "Break!" As quickly as the chase had started, it ended. He ran to the right and dropped to the ground and into the weeds out of sight, while Lopez pulled me to the left and back on the trail.

At this point, I'm thinking, what the hell just happened? Was that by chance or by design? It didn't take long to get the answer. My focus had shifted from thinking about ducks to this new challenge of chasing soldiers. We continued down the path and repeated the chase exercise another five times. As we finished the course I was thinking, "Interesting. They want me to scout soldiers, not ducks." I was still confused about the decoy terminology so maybe I had watched too much "National Geographic."

Lopez and I arrived back at the start area, and immediately he pulled the choke chain collar out of his pocket and put it back on me, switched to the leash from the scouting harness, and removed the harness, signaling that I was now off duty. He knelt down and wrapped his arm around my neck, a little too tight for my liking, and told me "Good boy, Chico, you did a great job!" I was thinking, what's your point? My favorite thing to do is go after people that get in my space and scare them half to death. Lopez walked me back to the stake-out area, and as he tied me up, he explained that he was going to get a bite to eat at the mess tent, and then had to finish up the day being a decoy. Suddenly I understood the decoy thing! If I had been able to talk, I would have told Lopez to watch his ass being a decoy, and I knew I smelled his lunch cooking when we arrived. Superhero talent!

Practice Makes Perfect

Over the following months we continued to follow a consistent routine. The handlers would talk about how they were up early and had to go to formations. They weren't wild about morning drills, feeling like they were back in Boot Camp and A.I.T. (Advance Infantry Training). I also learned, by listening to Lopez, why some of the uniforms were different. It turns out that a small number of the handlers were Marines training with the Army, which explained why some didn't like being called soldiers. They were Marines. Of course, I got that because I'm not wild about being called a dog. I'm an alpha husky shepherd and I'd like to get some respect!

Early each morning the handlers would arrive and pick us up and we would head out to one of the training areas. We would usually do some basic obedience drills to get us loosened up and get to know each other. Trust was important if we were going to be a team. I admit that I had some trust issues, being the first to be taken away from my mom. While feeling honored, I also felt like I was being abandoned. Living with Dave I felt like I overcame my abandonment issues and began trusting, until the meterman issue came up and I was shipped out to the Army. I'm going to be honest: I doubt if I will ever trust again. I worked with Lopez, but he didn't get my heart.

Our teams were broken up and often did different things in different areas. While one group would be on the scouting course, another might be doing basic obedience, or being exercised on an obstacle course. I wasn't big on basic obedience. Imagine that! But I loved scouting and the obstacle course.

Loving Obstacles

The thing I loved about the obstacle course was that I had the opportunity to improve my skills while working off excess energy. I see myself as basically honest, but I tend to hold back disclosing how I feel. It goes back to that trust thing. While I cry foul on some of the events of my life, I can own my part knowing I'm rather aggressive. Think about it from my perspective for a moment. Imagine that you get pulled away from not just one, but two families you love, and then find yourself with strangers. Imagine for a moment you're in the foster-care system moving from family to family, but you can't talk to anyone about it. Do you think you might be a little angry, afraid, or frustrated? Imagine also what it is like when you don't want to be hurt again and somebody gets in your space and you feel threatened. Do you think you might react in a way others may interpret as "crazy"? On top of that, imagine you have a ton of talent, but no one can see it and you can't speak. Imagine you want to tell them how special you are but your tongue is long and flat, keeping you from speaking. Do you think you might feel depressed because everyone around you thinks it's all about them and you're just there to serve them?

That's why I loved the obstacle course! I got to show the world some of the things I'm great at because, as a dog, it's all about show, not tell. I loved to zip through the course, through the pipes, up the ladders, over the walls, all while keeping my balance as I ran full speed down a seventy-five-foot telephone pole. When I finished, there was a sense of calm that came over me.

Sometimes I felt like the dog I once saw in a classic movie, *Old Yeller*. Old Yeller was playing the role of family protector like I was for Lisa. Eventually he was forced to defend the family against a rabid wolf, while my defense was against an unknown meterman. Old Yeller was bitten by the wolf, while I did the biting with the meterman. Because Old Yeller was exposed to rabies, he was now a threat to the family and the older son was forced to kill him. After the meterman event, I was a liability threat for Dave to be sued and he had to ship me off to the Army. In the end, like Old Yeller I just wanted to be a hero in someone's eyes and know that they weren't going to desert me because they thought I was too aggressive. I'm part husky, and that's what us husky Superheroes do!

A Familiar Decoy

I remember watching "National Geographic" on TV one evening and they went on and on about elephants and their unique abilities. What caught my attention was two particular things. One was that they can live up to sixty years. Now that's impressive. The second was not so impressive to me: they said the elephant has a great memory and if they are ever abused, there's a good chance they will seek revenge. I don't think that's unique to elephants. My case in point was the next day's scouting adventure. It was the highlight of my training so far. I had the routine down. My job was to signal Lopez that a decoy was ahead by giving some type of alert that he could recognize. Lopez's job was to recognize my alert and, according to its strength, calculate where the decoy was hiding by assessing wind speed, direction, and density of the terrain.

The decoy's job was to jump and run as I got close to him, to pique my interest in scouting humans. In my case we could have skipped this step as it's rather rudimentary, but for the flaky labs and high-strung shepherds training takes a little longer. Anyway, back to my point of the best day ever! Lo and behold, guess who was my third decoy? Remember the guy that I bit on his first day of feed detail? Decoy #3, up pops Monahan! When he jumped up and saw me, a look of terror was on his face. I wish I had a picture of that moment. In an instant he was off and running, and I was dragging Lopez to the point where he might have lost control of my leash. Monahan yelled, "Break!" but I didn't break as I continued to drag Lopez in hot pursuit of my target — Monahan. I didn't keep track, but I think there were four "Breaks" called out by Monahan before Lopez got the strength to pull me away. All I can remember is hearing Monahan's exhausted voice declare "Holy shit!" as he collapsed to the ground. I rest my case, and hope "National Geographic" does a series on huskie revenge and their memories. Maybe I have some elephant on my father's side!

Rumors of Vietnam

Over the next three months I was in scout-dog training at Fort Benning, and I must admit, my skills were honed significantly and my attitude softened. Once or twice I ran into Monahan and his dog, Rommel. After some observation I reconsidered and determined they were a good fit. From what I observed, Rommel was top-of-the-line when it came to intelligence. He was flexible and could sense a command was coming even before it was given. There was talk some of us would move on to off-leash scouting, where all the commands would be directed silently, with hand signals. In my opinion Rommel and I were the only two candidates with that kind of savvy!

There was talk of Vietnam among the troops, but it hadn't dawned on me up to that point we were preparing to go to Vietnam. The final month of training ramped up and got real as we switched to simulated Vietnam conditions. Now the obstacle course had trails leading into simulated Vietnamese villages, and the trails had various booby traps and I was expected to signal an alert so clearly that Lopez could learn how to stop a patrol. There were pits dug in the ground that were covered with branches and leaves as a trap for soldiers to fall into. I heard them tell the soldiers that in Vietnam they were called punji pits. They were filled with sharp bamboo stakes, sometimes with poison on the stakes to kill or injure soldiers who fall in. My job was to give Lopez early warnings so lives could be saved, and injuries avoided. The trainers also ran tripwires across the path and tied them to training explosives. Real explosives were used by the VC to set a trap and kill us Americans walking on the trails.

Once I knew the scope of my role and what was expected of me, I was confident and ready to help end the war in Vietnam. Specifically, I was to give early alerts so Lopez could warn the others in the patrol of eminent danger. I was also expected to keep an eye out and alert for tripwires and let him know if my super nose detected weapons or ammunition hidden by the enemy. Having watched the news with Dave helped me understand why we were doing so much training.

Superhero Bound

Early one morning, Lopez showed up looking a little stressed out and announced to me, "This is our big day, Chico. We are going to run an obstacle course and be graded." I was ready and raring to go, but Lopez didn't seem too confident, which sucks, because I will be graded on whether or not he recognizes my alerts. I made up my mind to just go and do what I'm expected to do and become the Superhero I was destined to be!

At about ten o'clock, Lopez put on my scouting harness; we were about to find out how we each did in learning our roles over the past three months. I'm certain you won't be surprised to hear that I aced the course. I alerted on four decoys, one tripwire, two punji pits and various hidden enemy weapons. While Lopez did well, he didn't fare as well as I, missing a few of my alerts and hitting the tripwire and one of the punji pits. Luckily, the scout dog training observer was seasoned and recognized my alerts and marked the failures on Lopez's section of the report card.

On that beautiful spring morning I was sitting erect next to Lopez's leg as he and the others stood at attention. The Bravo Company captain addressed our platoon, "Congratulations, men. You have completed the training and are certified scout dog handlers." And as quick as the formation started, it was over!

After the ceremony we broke into small groups where the platoon sergeants explained what would happen next. He said most but not all the dogs and handlers would be moving on to Vietnam. He told the men they would be given a thirty-day leave to go home and then report to Oakland, California, to fly out to Vietnam. He went on to explain that most of the dogs would be shipped to Vietnam and the teams would reunite, but if a member of the team wasn't there, a new team would be established.

Once everyone left for leave, we just hung around waiting to be shipped to Vietnam. That's when it began to sink in. I'm sure I maxed the final exam, so I thought I was on my way to Vietnam. But Lopez might not be there because of missing my alerts. That was the story of my life. Every time I thought I knew what to expect, the expected changed. Like now, as I am lying on this hot metal table waiting to be put down.

Leaving for Vietnam

Vietnam

After a couple of weeks hanging out at Fort Benning, the answer I awaited showed up in the form of a metal shipping cage. I was one of the dogs that had passed the final exam and was being loaded into a cage to be shipped to Vietnam. There were only a few dogs that remained tied up, and, Rommel, Monahan's dog, was being held back for further training. Like I said earlier, Rommel was top-notch, and my guess was they were putting him in that advanced off-leash program that some of the GI's had talked about during training. I believe the Army only has a select number of slots open for the off-leash positions. Maybe because the number of handlers was limited, I wasn't selected. Surely my performance qualified me to be in the program. In the short time I'd been in the Army, I'd learned that logical thinking isn't a common practice. There's always a surprise waiting around the corner.

The flight to Vietnam was unbelievably long. When I was watching the war coverage on TV, I guess I didn't pay much attention to where Vietnam is in relation to the United States. And now, thinking back, it makes sense. I would never have guessed in a million years I would ever leave Williston, North Dakota, much less end up in Vietnam in the Army! But there I sat, waiting for my turn to have a forklift unload me and my cage from the god-awful hot plane.

From all the films and commentaries, I had seen and heard on Vietnam and experiencing all the smells and the heat when we arrived, I knew this was my final stop. In all the specials on Vietnam where they interviewed soldiers, I had heard a common theme. First, the heat was unbearable; second, the monsoons seem like they would never end; and third, the collection of odd and strange smells were hard to describe. So, I assumed I was in Vietnam. The cage felt like it was cooking, and the scents that were coming through the cargo door told me there were hundreds of other things cooking in the hot outdoor sun. Finally, they off-loaded my cage and loaded all of us onto a truck.

There was no relief from the heat, so luckily it didn't take very long to get to our destination. I, along with twenty others, was delivered to what I found out later was the in-country Scout Dog Pickup Kennels in Long Binh. It was the place the Army scout dogs were sent to be later joined by their handlers. While it was hot, it was better than being in a cage on the plane or traveling on a truck. I decided to relax and take it easy, sensing things were going to ramp up quickly.

I spent the next few days lying around on the cool concrete of my kennel trying to pick up any breeze that might pass by. Some designated soldier fed us once a day. While it wasn't like Momma used to serve, it wasn't too bad. Twice a day someone would come by with a hose and squirt down our kennels to clean up the mess we had made while being confined to the three-foot by eight-foot kennel. I love a clean kennel, and the bonus was the water cooled the concrete even more so I could relax. Life is relative. What you think is awful one moment may feel like a blessing the next moment. So, I was thinking how good I had it, lying there on the damp concrete floor instead of being in a cramped cage on a plane, puddle-jumping the ocean on a twenty-hour flight. But as I was lying there relaxing, I couldn't help but feeling sad as my memory drifted back to hanging out with Lisa and playing fetch with her. I could hear her squeaking my favorite blue bone toy. What I would have given to be lying in front of the TV and watching coverage of the Vietnam War instead of being here in person. Isn't perspective a wonderful thing?

Time is a funny thing too. When you're busy, it seems you never have enough time, but when you're not busy, it seems you have too much time. Lying around felt like I had way too much time. Having all those days to myself with nothing to do was fun at first, but eventually it got rather uncomfortable. For me, self-talk started out with just, "Chill, Chico." Then I got into worrying about what was going to happen, and before I knew it, I was worried about something in the future that might not happen until after I'm dead. By the way, I liked to worry! Then after I wear myself out worrying, I begin to adjust and think about the good old days. The short time I spent with Mom and my siblings didn't last long, but it's one of my top memories. I was connected, I was loved, and I was safe. Next on my list was when Dave said I was special and picked me up from my blanket and announced that my name was Chico. That was my first life-changing event. I was connected to a new family who could not only show me love but could speak to me and tell me how much they loved me. I was safe and helped keep the family safe. As I said, those early years were the best years for me. All that Army down-time sure had the wheels turning in my head. I hated to discount Lopez, but that was a short working relationship with not much time to get to know each other well during our hectic three-month schedule. He was a good enough guy, but not to be a good enough memory.

The Handlers Are Here

My kennel was about fifteen feet down from the main entrance to the holding complex. Even so, I was one of the last to find out what was going on. But I knew something was brewing when the chain-reaction barking began. You see, there are different barks. When one dog barks, most of the pack will follow suit. Now if you have ten dogs barking, but nine of the ten aren't sure what they are barking at or about, I call it mob-barking. I'm not much of a mob barker. I don't like wasting my energy. If you listen closely, you can hear the tone change when a dog moves from mob-barking to now-I-see-why-I'm-barking-barking. It's way more assertive and aggressive. We aren't much different from humans. I can remember times when Dave and Sandy would have a disagreement and their voice tones would go up in pitch. But as the argument went on, it would sometimes break into a shouting contest, thus shifting from mob-barking to "Now I know what is pissing me off."

That morning I awoke to mob-barking, but I could tell there was a lot of activity because things were moving in a frenzy. Then I got to see what was going on firsthand. Soldiers started passing my cage door looking for their dog. All the commotion piqued my attention and I stood up to look for Lopez. Several handlers passed my cage door but not Lopez. Then it happened. Hold on — there's a familiar face! It was my buddy Monahan, and he recognized me too. It's funny the way we remember good friends and good enemies. He and I made eye contact and acknowledged one another. Eventually all the activity ended, and the handlers left the kennel. Once again it was time for me to relax, reflect, and worry about my status. Lopez wasn't there. Again, hurry up and wait!

I took a quick snooze and once again was awakened by mob-barking. The next thing I knew the handlers were taking their dogs out of the kennels for a walk. I was thinking at the time, "Man, what I'd give to get out of here and bleed off a little energy!" That's when it happened: Monahan appeared right in front of my cage door and reached for the latch. I was thinking, "I can't believe he's going to venture into my space," because I can smell fear on a human and Monahan was stinking to high heaven. So being the king of set-ups, I started wagging my tail to lure him into a false sense of security. And it worked! He stepped in and locked the gate behind him. I was wagging away, so he bent down and started to pet me. Now, I must admit I love to have fingers run through my fur, and it had been a long time since I had been around anyone and had been touched. Monahan continued to pet me and play around for about ten minutes, and I lapped it up. I was enjoying his company, but when he finished, the old Chico showed up. As he turned to walk out, I bit him in the ass! I thought, "That will teach you to never assume a tail-wagging dog is your friend!" Believe me, there are times I don't even understand why I do the things I do that get me in trouble!

Jerk and Bite

The next week was set aside for basic obedience and exercise for the dog teams. For us it was a basic battle of the wills to see who was going to be in charge. Every time Monahan gave me a command, I would ignore him. Then he would jerk me with the leash hooked to the choke chain collar and I would bite him in return. I figured it was a battle of the wills and I was an alpha-willed dog! There were times when I got a little more out of control — imagine that! And he would apply a swinging technique to keep me from lunging and biting him. It took a few days before we both got tired of fighting each other and came to a non-verbal agreement: I wouldn't bite him when he gave me a command, but I still got to growl at all commands. Once we'd made that agreement, we began to relax, hang out, and do a little bonding. By the way, the no-bite agreement was an exclusive arrangement between me and PFC Monahan. I reserved the right, at will, to bite anyone else that violated my personal space.

Over that week, we got to know each other a little better. We were housed close to the airfield where we had landed when we arrived in country. Each day there were two flights that arrived with new recruits and would later leave with soldiers who had finished their tour in Vietnam and were headed for home. At the airport I got to witness one of the arrivals, and it was a very emotional exchange to watch. The soldiers waiting to board the return flight were cheering as the incoming soldiers were getting off the plane. I was thinking it was very cool to see them support each other, but later overheard two of the soldiers discussing how excited they were to see the plane. Then it dawned on me that they weren't applauding the new recruits. They were applauding the plane, their ticket back home, or back to "The World" as they called it.

The contrast between those getting off the plane and those getting on was dramatic. The arriving troops had crisp green uniforms and their faces were alive with the look of fear and dismay. On the other hand, the soldiers returning to "The World" were in dirty, faded fatigues, and while they were excited to be going home, most looked like they had been awake for days. Most of the soldiers had blank stares on their faces, like the lights are on but nobody's home! I can tell you, even I was taken aback when I saw those 200 warriors, exhausted but alive and going home. I thought, "Now I get what they were talking about on the news." In that moment, I was wondering how I would look in a year from now when I was heading home, if I was lucky enough to make it. Now that I think of it, they never loaded any dogs on the planes returning home.

This is when things started to change between Monahan and me. There was an early morning flight and an evening flight. In the morning we were busy exercising and practicing commands and obedience training when the plane approached for landing. I would notice Monahan pausing to watch the flight land and later take off. He always had a strange look on his face. The other flight was late afternoon, about an hour before feeding time. Monahan would come get me and we would go for a walk and he would talk to me. When the plane would approach and begin to land, he would kneel and confide in me. I think he believed I didn't understand, and I was a safe ear for him to talk to.

That's when our relationship started to change and I decided to give in and refer to him by his first name, Mike.

Mike was young and I could tell he was afraid and, like many of the other handlers and me, homesick already! He would say, "Chico, I have to change my attitude! If I believe I'm going to die here, I will. I have to decide I'm going to be the best scout dog handler I can be and trust that God will protect me." He would talk to me about us never working together, but shortly afterwards we would be leading patrols. He was wondering out loud if I were good at scouting and questioning how long it would take before he recognized my alerts. It all started to hit me. Mike and I were a lot alike. We were both afraid we weren't prepared to face what lay ahead, and we both missed home and felt alone.

This is where I got frustrated being a dog. If I could only speak, I could have eased many of Mike's fears. I had aced the final exam at Fort Benning, and I knew what I was doing. Mike cleared up some of my confusion in one of our evening chats, because he talked about how much he missed Rommel, and how Rommel had had an intestinal bug going into exam week. He said Rommel was a stellar dog, and because he was sick, he missed a couple of trip wires, and that's probably why he wasn't waiting here in Vietnam. Mike was very gracious when he was sharing about Rommel. I never once felt like Mike was saying he was disappointed in partnering with me. He just was expressing his respect for Rommel and his abilities. After I ate later that evening, lying in my kennel and reflecting on the day, I admitted I was shocked to find myself getting attached to Mike. I had sworn I wasn't going to trust anyone again. I guess that's what I get for swearing!

The 46th Scout Dog Platoon

The 46th Scout Dog Platoon, 26th Infantry, Tay Ninh

After a week or so, a truck arrived to take Mike and me to our assigned destination, the 46th Scout Dog Platoon (46th IPSD) with the 25th Infantry Division, in Tay Ninh. I was looking forward to getting settled in and doing some scouting. Since Dave had dropped me off, I felt like I'd been around the world, probably because I had!

The ride to the 46th took a couple of hours on a hot, bumpy, and dusty road. As I bounced around in my cage it hit me once again. This is it. I was in Vietnam and life was going to be much more difficult than what I had been accustomed to. I started thinking about all the news coverage and wondering what I would experience. Would I be patrolling in dense jungle, or zigzagging across rice paddy dikes? Would I be slogging through water during the monsoon season or be up in the mountain region capturing some hill that only had a number for a name, like Hill 392? Do they just assign a number to each hill? My imagination was alive with all the possibilities. Eventually we arrived at our new home, and Mike took me out of the cage, and we headed over to see my new accommodations.

I guess you might say I received a warm welcome. As Mike walked me down the main aisle that separates the cages in the kennel, there were several dogs barking at me, mainly mob-barking. I was home and it was just a little more of what it'd been, a six-by-ten foot cage with concrete floor and walls up five feet, with a chain-link fence the rest of the way up, a corrugated metal roof, and a chain-link gate with a down hasp. It wasn't the Ritz, but it got me out of the sweltering sun.

Once I got settled in, I could see there was a daily routine. Some of the handlers and their dogs would be out in the field for five days at a time and then return for a couple of days. People were rotating in and out of the field daily, and there were twenty-four dog teams, including us, at the 46th IPSD. When the GI's were in from the field, they would have morning formation and be assigned different clean-up or maintenance details to perform.

My favorite part of the day was when I got to spend some time with Mike on the obstacle course. It was perfectly set up to challenge all my skills: horizontal ladders and telephone poles to test my balance, and vertical ladders to test my climbing abilities. It had plenty of walls to jump over and windows to jump through, but sadly no screen doors. Just kidding! There were culvert pipes positioned close to the ground to challenge and test my willingness to low-crawl in confined conditions. Whoever designed this course had a dog's mind, because they even put in a fake fire plug for us to leave our calling card. That piece-of-metal fire plug carried the scents of many a fine scout dog, past and present, at the 46th!

So anyway, each day when we were at our barracks in base camp, Mike would run me through the course to exercise me and throw in a few commands. This is where we started to define our boundaries and agreements better. For example, I would be on a full-blown run and he'd yell, "Stop!" and I'd stop. Next he'd say, "Sit," and I would resist! He would raise his voice and say "Sit!" I would respond by growling at him. He would then say, "You better sit," and I would slowly sit while growling at him the whole time. This was the routine exercise we played while not in the field, so we each knew where the other stood. We had to be able to trust each other when we were leading patrols in the field — when it was a life-and-death situation.

The other thing I liked is rather ironic when I think back on how Mike and I met, him trying to feed me and me biting him. Now what I loved was Mike pampering me, squirting out my kennel, bringing me fresh water to drink a couple times a day, and, most of all, his preparing my food and serving it to me each evening. I felt special!

This routine went on for about two weeks, and then everything changed again.

The Obstacle Course – My Favorite Thing to Do

Jumping got me ready for action.

Focused on Staying Alive.

Mike teaching me to jump.

Low Crawl Training.

Ladders and poles
were perfect for my
agility training.

Some off-leash time with Mike.

Going to War

One morning Mike showed up at my door in full gear, steel pot on his head, rucksack on his back, canteens of water on one shoulder, an M16 slung over the other, and bandoleers of ammunition magazines across his chest. "Time to go, boy," he said to me. He slid the choke chain over my ears and around my neck, hooked a six-foot leash to my collar and we were off. We hopped into the company jeep, and a fellow dog handler drove us about five minutes to a helicopter pad where chopper flights flew in and out of the Tay Ninh Base Camp.

We exited the jeep and were greeted by one of the air controllers. I knew this soldier was a smart man because the first words out of his mouth were, "Good looking dog you got there, Dog Man. What's his name? Is it okay to pet him?" Mike instinctively snapped the leash, my cue to sit in the heel position, and responded, "Thanks. His name is Chico, and I would suggest you keep your distance. He has been known to bite quite a few people." The controller backed up and responded, "Got it. Your chopper is loaded and ready to take you and some supplies to Fire Base Charlie."

And with that we walked over to the chopper with the blades already whirling, and the crew chief signaled us onto the chopper. I had been on a few airplanes, but this was my first helicopter ride. I was so fired up about what was about to happen that when I sat down in the chopper it hit me, I should have taken a pee. What was I thinking?

Mike was sitting in the seat that almost looked like a fold-out cot and was keeping me tightly held close to his knee. His hand was on the buckle of the leash and the ring it attached to on my collar. As the chopper lifted off, I began to scope out the terrain. It was my job to pay attention. I saw there were two pilots up front flying the chopper and a door gunner off to my right. That was it. Just the five of us.

This was different from the films I'd seen on the news. In those clips I remember them flying in groups of eight, and they would have extra fire support helicopters for protection. But this was us, all alone. This experience was way different from being in a plane. Even though I had a vivid imagination, this first flight exceeded any and all expectations I had prior to flying. What I remember most about my first flight was looking down at the rice paddies and seeing how green and beautiful this country was, despite the ongoing war.

We were in the air for about twenty minutes before we began to descend. With both side doors wide open, I could see a small round circle in the distance. I was expecting to see a base camp like Tay Ninh. I was thinking, "This surely can't be Fire Base Charlie. It's way too small!" Two minutes later we set down on a small helipad outside of Fire Base Charlie, a small, round, fortified circle in the middle of nowhere. This was our new home base for the next five days.

The first thing I noticed was that the fire base was surrounded by several layers of barbed wire and rolls of concertina wire to ward off enemy attacks and infiltrators like the VC and NVA. They had pulled back a section of wire for us to enter the compound, and the next thing that caught my attention was the amount of artillery in the bunker line. This place was ready and equipped to do some fighting! One of the platoon leaders directed us to a small bunker and told Mike to stow his gear, tie me up, and join him for a briefing at 16:00 hours in the command bunker.

Mike introduced himself to a couple of the guys in the bunker and told them my name and warned them against getting too close to me. They chuckled and acknowledged the warning. Mike picked a shaded spot right outside the bunker, tied me up, and gave me some chow and water. Then he went to the briefing. That evening was pretty relaxed. I could hear artillery and small weapons fire and saw a couple of flares lighting up the night sky off in the distance. Other than a few noises from the changing of the guards, I got a good night's sleep.

First Patrol

The sun was up early and so were we. Fire Base Charlie was alive with activity. Everyone seemed to be hustling to get things ready for the day's mission. Mike had already gone over to the command bunker for an early-morning briefing and was back gathering up some gear. The good news for him, I guess, was that it looked like we would only be out for the day, so he didn't have to carry five days of food and water for both of us, which I'm sure is exceptionally heavy.

Mike appeared from inside the bunker with minimal gear. He was wearing a hat, no steel pot, his M16 and extra ammo, a canteen of water, and my scouting harness. That's it! He hooked the six-foot leash to my choke collar, and we joined the rest of the platoon in the field outside the wire. There were eight groups of soldiers spaced out in the field, and the platoon sergeant told us which group to join and where to stand. Mike looked rather nervous, but my ears told me what was about to happen.

I was right! I heard the deep sound of rotor blades churning off in the distance, and suddenly they appeared! I saw the Eagle Flight approaching — eight Huey choppers (Slicks, as they were called) flying in formation, four side-by-side to pick us up, an LOH (Light Observation Helicopter) in the lead flying at tree-top level, and two Cobras (heavy weapon helicopters) hovering high above the formation, ready to provide instant fire support for the mission if needed. Once you hear an Eagle Flight arrive, it's a sound that you will never forget, especially when you are under attack. In that case, the sound of them coming in was a blessing.

The eight slicks landed, and we were the first to jump on our chopper. Mike held me in close once again and had me jump on board. He sat down at the entrance with his legs hanging out of the chopper and his feet right over the landing skids. He had me on a tight leash between him and the door gunner, keeping me away from the other grunts (soldiers) getting on the chopper. Quickly we were airborne, and the wind blowing across my face caused a potpourri of smells to fill my nose. You talk about a wild ride! Here I was, sitting on the edge of the door opening of a helicopter, thousands of feet in the air, trusting that Mike, whom I'd mistreated, wasn't going to throw me out to my death, and give it an "Oops! He slipped out of my hands!" From that time forward I worked a little harder to build a better relationship with Mike and began trusting him. After all, our lives depended on each other.

As we flew over South Vietnam, I noticed that it looked more scenic than a war zone. Before I knew it, the slicks touched down in the middle of some rice paddies, and Mike and I were the first ones out of the chopper. The rest of the soldiers jumped off immediately. The choppers were only on the ground for a few seconds and flew off. I later learned that choppers are most vulnerable to enemy attack when sitting on the ground.

Once the area was secure, the platoon sergeant and captain came up to fill us in on the mission and direction of the patrol. Finally, I felt like a member of the team. I was given the respect I deserved and was included in the mission briefing. Mike put on my scouting harness and told them we were ready when they were, and in one minute we were walking point (leading the patrol). We were officially on our first combat mission. I was so excited; to think there were a hundred lives depending on me to deliver an early alert on the enemy. As we wove our way, zigzagging across the dikes of the rice paddy, there was a gentle breeze in our favor, coming directly toward us. Wind is tricky when it comes to smells. If it shifts for a moment and I pick up a scent, Mike had better be paying attention to the direction of the wind at that exact moment of my alert so he could identify the exact location of the enemy. A missed alert could leave the entire company of men vulnerable and open to walk into an ambush and be killed. I took my job seriously and hoped Mike did the same.

We patrolled for about six hours that day with no enemy contact — all in all, a good day for our first time on patrol. The heat was staggering, the humidity was high, and the rice paddies put off a stench that could challenge the fine tuning of a nose even as good as mine. All this took some getting used to, right down to the water Mike gave me. It was warm and had that plastic canteen smell that transferred to the taste of the water and ruined the experience of a fresh, cool lap of water.

The long hot day of patrolling was over, and we were told to take our positions and prepare to be picked up. Once again, with my superpowers I could hear the helicopters coming before they could be seen. About that time the platoon sergeant popped a canister of yellow smoke to mark our pickup zone. Within minutes the Eagle Flight touched down to pick us up and return us to Fire Base Charlie, our home base for the remaining four days with Charlie Company. Chow that evening was like eating cardboard. Mike had packed my food for our five days in the field. I realized everything was designed to be lightweight because he had to carry all his equipment, plus mine, but I think someone could have been a little more creative with the taste and texture of my field rations. But then I guess I can't complain. The C-rations Mike and the rest of the troops had to eat in the field were no better than what I was getting.

That evening is when it all hit me. Mike and I were an exclusive, two-man, dog team! Sitting there by our bunker together was rather odd. The men of Charlie Company were all around us, but hardly anyone acknowledged our presence. From their perspective we were there to lead their patrol. You might say we were hired guns, not a part of their company. As much as I wanted to fight trusting Mike, he and I were a team, and based on our past relationship failures, I knew I needed to let go and get closer to him. I could see in his eyes that he was lonely, and I could smell the fear on his body. That's the thing humans don't get. We can read their feelings with uncanny accuracy. Part of trusting him was selfish on my part. If Mike's fear caused him to miss an alert, he could get all of us killed. I knew I would deliver Superhero results while on patrol, but I needed to help Mike be at his best, so we wouldn't die in that godforsaken place.

The next four days we boarded the choppers and patrolled all day, returning to Fire Base Charlie each evening. Each day brought new experiences and opportunities to learn. Mike and I were now learning how to be the best dog team ever, through experiencing action on daily patrols and spending evenings bonding together. Mike would have conversations with me about personal stuff he was dealing with because of being here in Vietnam. I quickly realized there were a lot of issues to cover. For one, I was surprised to see how diverse the terrain was that we flew over, just to get to the location that we were going to patrol. We spent a couple of days patrolling areas around rice paddies, then around small villages, and sometimes we patrolled intensely thick jungle terrain. It was so thick I could barely pick up a scent to work my magic.

Before I knew it, our first week in the field was over. Mike gathered up our gear and we got ready to return to Tay Ninh Base Camp. Soon a supply chopper arrived with some supplies, mail for the soldiers, and another dog team to replace us. Once everything was unloaded, we were signaled to board and off we went back to the 46th Scout Dog Platoon. Oddly enough, it felt good to be back in my concrete kennel, eating some regular food and lapping up some fresh water — "home, sweet home!"

Rest and Exercise

I guess I had this idea in my mind that when we weren't in the field on patrol Mike and I would be spending our days together, but that didn't happen. Every morning the handlers would go to breakfast and return to morning formation. The platoon sergeant would assign each of them a detail for the day. Some guys worked on the company truck and jeep, others would clean up areas around the sleeping barracks, and others would have kennel clean-up detail. This kept the dog handlers busy most of the day, while most of my time was spent lying around watching platoon activity through the chain-link fence of my kennel.

Two of the most exciting events of the day for me were chow time and exercise hour, when Mike would come to my kennel and take me to the obstacle course. I was excited to get out of my cage, and I loved to run through all the obstacles. The first few times I ran the course, I found it to be challenging, but with a little practice, I found my confidence. The course was set up to challenge and hone the skills needed by us scout dogs, and Mike would run me through it over and over again. I loved it and we had a lot of fun together. It was a great opportunity for Mike and me both to blow off some steam, work out our differences, and get clear on how our relationship was going to work.

I was a big enough dog to admit that I was a little bit stubborn, and I hoped Mike could admit he was stubborn too. Stubborn always seems to play out in the form of power and control. I admit I didn't like being told what to do, and it was obvious Mike didn't like it either. I think we were put together to work on letting go of control and learning the benefits of cooperation, lessons that showed up as we did the elements of the exercise course. Each element revealed a challenge for us to work on in our relationship. I decided base camp was the safest place to work on our disagreements, not out on patrol where so many lives were in our hands.

At some point, I realized that the obstacle course was also an arena for Mike and me to build trust. My story is simple. While I see myself as a loyal dog, somehow that has gotten me in the so-called doghouse with my owners. It's tough to trust once you feel like trust in a relationship has been betrayed. This relationship with Mike was different. We were together in an everyday life-and-death situation. When we were not in the field walking point, facing the enemy, we were in base camp getting rocketed every night. While the handlers could hunker down in their bunkers, we dogs were left in our kennels with little or no protection.

The soldier's bunkers were often dug into the ground and covered with sandbags. I got it that Mike cared about me, but there's a military attitude that was apparent. The military saw me as expendable equipment, not as a soldier. Yes, there were some rules about treatment in our favor, but we weren't held in high enough esteem for the job we were doing. I was there to save American lives and the Army acted like I was just a dog, not a highly trained professional. I wanted to scream sometimes, "I'm a soldier, not somebody's pet!" Since I couldn't scream, I could have barked or howled, but that's not a good move for a scout dog on patrol.

In the meantime, I loved the change of attitude that Mike had made. He definitely knew that I knew my stuff as a scout dog, and he trusted me. I'd sworn I'd never trust anyone again, but I think I broke my promise. Mike and I were a team, and trust was paramount to our staying alive.

Rest and exercise didn't last very long for us. Mike ran off his mouth and got into an argument with the platoon sergeant the first day we were there. That meant we were sent into the field quicker and more often than most of the other dog teams. The sergeant denied that he was sending us out earlier and more often, and Mike countered with thanking him, saying, "You're doing me a favor. I will either get killed early and get it over with, or later, after you are gone, I'll be the first off-line (no longer patrolling) for having the most days in the field." It was Mike's way of growling and letting that sergeant know he couldn't control Mike's attitude!

Walking Point in A Pointless War

Life often works in strange ways. When faced with change I seem to have conflicting emotions. On one paw I feel fearful not knowing what's about to happen, while on the other paw, I feel excited about the possibility of new adventures. Looking back seems to work much the same. When I was a pup and with my mom and brothers and sisters, I felt safe and loved. Then people started to arrive, looking at us as potential pets. I was confused and afraid at the same time. When Dave first picked me up, I'll never forget the feeling of his hands on my stomach, very gentle, but a feeling of strength, too. When I realized I wouldn't be going back to my mom and the rest of the litter, the conflicting feelings began. I was proud that I was chosen by Lois to be a gift to her brother, but I was sad that I might never see my mom or my family again. And I was excited that I was getting to go explore a whole new world.

Once I was with Dave and the new family, all my attention moved to the new adventures, and what a learning experience that time with them was for me! But with that one decision to protect Lisa, my life abruptly changed forever. As Mike and I prepared to head back out to face the enemy, I began to realize that life was always changing and my job was to figure out what I needed to do to become a Superhero. Waiting for Mike, I was crystal clear about my role in my new adventure, and was excited and determined that I, alpha

Chico, was going to stand out as top dog in the 46th Scout Dog Platoon pack. Watch for me in the news! Then Mike interrupted my thoughts saying, "Come on, boy. We need to get moving. The chopper is waiting to take us to our next adventure."

The company clerk dropped us off at the airfield to grab our chopper flight to the next fire base where we would find out our new assignment. I was starting to feel like a General: we had a driver and a jeep to drive us, and a private chopper pilot to take us to our destination. Of course, I quickly returned to reality the next morning when we were slogging through rice paddies and chopping through the jungles of Vietnam. But for a moment, I enjoyed my delusion.

As we approached the flight line, I heard a familiar voice say, "Hey, you two are back! And, yes, I know, don't pet that fine-looking dog, Chico!" Wow! I was impressed. The air traffic controller we had met last week remembered us, and — not bragging — he called only me by name. Mike's name wasn't even mentioned. By the way, here's another thing that humans do that drives me crazy. They always refer to us as their dog first. I know I'm a dog and you know I'm a dog, so why not skip a step and just ask, "What's his name?" I know this is just my "pet" peeve, no pun intended, but I never heard anybody say to a friend with a new acquaintance, "What's your human's name?" And yes, I do realize that when I'm nervous, like before a mission, I find distractions to take my mind off my fears, with biting people being one of my favorite ways to create some chaotic distraction.

Soon we were on the chopper headed out for five days of sun and fun in Vietnam. I could never have imagined back in the old "evening news" days that I would find myself in an Army helicopter fighting in the Vietnam War. But there I was, looking down at my next assignment.

This fire base looked different from the one where we were the week before. The chopper touched down outside the wire and we jumped off. A soldier greeted us and took us to the command bunker. Mike tied me up and went inside for a meeting while I scoped out my new surroundings. Quickly I assessed what the difference was that I recognized from the air. This is where watching the news all those nights paid off.

I remember watching Walter Cronkite reporting on the use of tanks in Vietnam. He didn't call them tanks. He said they were called an APC, an Army Personnel Carrier, and went on to explain why the soldiers were riding on top and not inside. He said that the APC was designed to transport troops inside, but because the roads were mined by the VC, everyone sat on top to avoid getting killed if they hit a mine. Everyone, that is, except the driver, who stood inside with his head sticking out. I was excited and could hardly wait for Mike to come out and brief me on his meeting. I hoped I would get to ride on top of an APC just like Walter Cronkite had described. Finally, the briefing was over, and the suspense was killing me. Mike said, "Come on, boy. Let's get settled into our new luxury accommodations."

Life in the fire support base was more difficult than back in the Tay Ninh Base Camp. The reality was that what cover we had was for Mike, not me. His sleeping area was unbelievable. They took old wooden ammunition boxes and placed them on the ground to create a space for a soldier to lie down. On top of the ammo boxes they put a half of a metal culvert pipe and finished it off with layers of sandbags. It was the Vietnam War version of an igloo, I guess. At night

Mike would lie down and slide under the pipe, then pull me in to protect us both from the incoming rocket attacks that were frequent events.

It was moments like that, when I was in unfamiliar surroundings and feeling a little lonely, that I had the urge to take off and run back home. It's one of my old habits. While trying to get to sleep, I began to think about the last time I tried to run back home. It was when Dave took the new job in Williston, not too far away from that cute little house in Tioga, North Dakota. As I said earlier, when Dave, Lisa, and Sandy packed up, I figured I was part of the family and would move with them, but to my surprise Dave dropped me off at a local farmer's home.

Now don't get me wrong the old farmer was a nice man. He fed me well and let me run loose in one of the large, fenced pastures. I figured it would only be a few days, and after the family got settled in, they would be back to pick me up to rejoin them. Well, days turned into weeks and I was getting restless. It was time for me to make a break for freedom. I was falling behind on current events, not having a TV, so I knew I had to take charge. The great thing about old farms is they aren't always maintained, and you can find a hole in the fence here and there. With that thought, I headed out through a hole in the south pasture and headed back to the home in Tioga. I knew the family wouldn't be there, but I figured that someone would figure out how to get ahold of Dave for me. Luckily, the walk wasn't all that far, and the anticipation of my whole adventure piqued my interest and distracted my attention away from walking. I will never forget the feeling of comfort that overtook me when I arrived and lay down on the front porch, safely home again.

Of course, all good things must come to an end, including this. I guess it was the new owner who showed up and told me to get out of there. As you can imagine, I just had to tell him how I felt about that, so I showed him a mouth full of teeth and a big growl. I had made up my mind that I wasn't going anywhere. I was going to lie on this porch until Dave came to pick me up and take me to their new home to join Lisa and Sandy. Life can be amazing when you make up your mind and stick to your guns. It only took two nights and several more "Get outta here's" before a policeman showed up and told the owner that he recognized me and knew my owner. He gave Dave a call, and, just like that, Dave was there, shaking his head and putting me in the car. But even though I had that urge again, to cut and run was not an option in Vietnam.

Anyway, to continue my story, that night I was restless. Mike was quiet, the mosquitoes were terrible, and the heat was unbearable. We got rocketed, and there was a lot of small arms fire around the perimeter, so flares were lighting up the sky all around us most of the evening. Finally, it was daybreak, and soon I learned what we were to do that day. Mike had been hush-mouthed about our mission, which had me feeling like I wasn't part of the team, and I hated that feeling.

Mike was up at the break of dawn and headed over to the command bunker for the morning briefing. I found it hard to believe that there were no canine representatives at the morning briefings. I was walking point, leading the patrol, with everyone's life depending on my superpowers, and they didn't have the courtesy to include me. There is an underlying military attitude that ignores the value of the work that military dogs perform. I think it goes back to the civilian idea that we are domesticated and intended to perform as pets.

I think humans will one day learn to respect our abilities to detect almost anything, well beyond hunting birds and rabbits. One day you will see assist dogs in every area — criminal justice, drug detection, medical and disease detection, to name a few. This is my big complaint about having a flat tongue for lapping water. I would gladly trade it in for one that allowed me to speak. It's just my speculation, but I believe that if I could speak, I would probably have little need to bite people. Just think how it feels to be unable to communicate information that is critical for others, or for me not to be able to express my opinions. Not being able to talk would make anyone aggressive!

Okay, once again I'm on my soap box because I have too much alone time. I'd better hurry and finish my story before they come to put me down.

Mike returned from the command bunker and put on his gear, hooked the six-foot leash on my choke chain, and said, "Chico, are you ready for a new adventure?" The next thing I heard was several APC's starting up and lining up at the main entrance.

"Okay, boy. We are going to be riding today. This is a Mechanized Unit (APC) and we are going out to secure the main highway so the convoys can safely deliver supplies." I was thinking this was a little odd because what am I going to do? The platoon leader yelled out, "Dog Man, you are on track number three," and with that, we went to the third APC to await further direction. The driver, with his head sticking out of the hatch, told Mike, "You and your dog climb on board and you can sit on the fence."

To my surprise, Mike lifted me up and pushed me on top of the APC; then he climbed up to join me. At the rear on top was a roll of chain-link fence where Mike sat down with me between his legs. There were about six other guys on top with us. This seemed like a very dangerous way to travel. There was the obvious potential of falling off, or a sniper picking us off. But before I knew it, we were off and moving down the highway. Mike asked a bunch of questions, and I finally got to hear what the hell was going on.

One of the guys explained the reason for the chain-link fence. He said if they had to set-up outside of the fire base at night, the fence would surround the APC. He told us the VC often fired RPG's (rocket-propelled grenades) at the APC, but the rockets would explode when they hit the fence, keeping them from hitting the APC. One mystery solved. He said what we were doing was routine for them because the roads had to be cleared of land mines and trip wires every morning. Once they finished sweeping the road, the Mech Unit was deployed to establish security for the convoys traveling the highway.

Eventually all my questions were answered. The guy told Mike that we were headed for a rubber-tree plantation next to the highway, and we had to patrol the area to make sure there were no VC setting up as snipers to attack the convoy. I thought my rides in metal shipping crates were bad, but this was worse. The easy part was sitting atop the hot tank crowded with soldiers traveling down the highway at 40mph. The difficult part of the trip for me was listening to the metal tracks on blacktop, singing a tune that would surely render me deaf. This was not music to my sensitive ears. Mike was right, it was truly a new adventure.

Every time the two of us were in the field, I listened closely and tried to understand the entire picture of what made men tick in war. This first outing with a mechanized unit was a little chaotic on so many levels, but over the year I learned what was really happening. In the beginning the APC drivers would all come to Mike and ask us to ride on their track (APC). I felt proud, thinking they wanted the honor of our presence. Eventually my Superhero ego was deflated when I heard one of the track drivers tell Mike why he wanted us on-board. As it turns out, the ARVN's (South Vietnamese Army) would join us on patrol, and to say they were chaotic would be a gigantic understatement. They would be talking at a hundred miles an hour, carrying their M16's across their shoulders like a yoke on a water buffalo. The driver told Mike, "Ride with us, Dog Man, because the Vietnamese are afraid of your dog and won't ride with us." So, there you have it. Dog teams were nothing more than a good deterrent from transporting ARVN troops who were really disliked by infantry soldiers and infantry mechanized units.

The exception to the rule was when the APC's had to navigate rice paddies. One of the first times out I got to experience the ride of my life! When the APC travels over a dike, it's like walking up a teeter-totter. The front of the APC stands straight up, then it levels off for a second, and suddenly the nose flops down and the tail end flips up like a catapult. Some of the drivers would invite the ARVN's on board their APC knowing that they would sit on the roll of fence on top and to the rear of the APC. Eventually the patrol would have to cross the rice paddies, and after crossing a couple of dikes slowly the driver would announce in English, "Hold on, boys." The ARVN's would be running their mouths and not many spoke English, so they did not heed the warning. At that point, the driver would begin his ascent slowly, but instead of continuing slowly to step two of leveling out, he would gun the engine, flipping the APC forward and catapulting the unsuspecting ARVN's through the air like the Flying Wallendas falling off their tight wire.

While I must admit this was somewhat mean-spirited, it was so funny to watch. Now I can appreciate all I learned watching TV "back in the world" with Dave. He knew I loved to watch diverse shows to continue to stay active in current events. The Flying Wallendas' tragedy was before my time, but if my memory serves me, two of the members of their family fell to their deaths from a tight wire strung high atop two buildings back in 1962 in Chicago. I must smile inside when I think about all this. I was lucky that Dave gave me to the Army and not a high-wire act in some circus. Learning to walk on a high wire, even for a Superhero like me, would be a challenge. Oh well, back to business.

When you are in a war, far away from home, and think you are going to die, all the old rules drop off. There was a lot of resentment directed by US soldiers toward the ARVN's. I totally understand the mistrust. We were over here fighting a war for a cause most of us didn't understand, while their own soldiers were unprofessional and often put us in more jeopardy. Mike and I did spend a week with an Airborne ARVN Unit and they totally had it together, so all their troops weren't bad. But when you have buddies who are killed, and the people you work with look the same as the enemy, and many are enemy sympathizers, it's easy to allow hatred and mistrust to take over. The benefit that Mike and I had was getting to go back to base camp every five days and get our heads straight, so to speak. You may never really get your head straight in war, but we learned to appreciate the moments when we were not in imminent danger.

The thing about walking point is you are always in imminent danger of being killed. Mike was twenty-one and I was three, the same age in dog years as Mike. We were two youngsters who had never imagined we would be in that hideous war doing one of its most dangerous jobs. When that finally sank in, I realized I faced my toughest challenge: trusting someone to have my back, no matter what happened.

I've been a fighter from the beginning, and that has played out in ways that have sabotaged some of the good experiences in my life. Looking back, I can see my part in Dave's decision to donate me to the military, but that doesn't squelch my feeling of being abandoned. When I look at my relationship with Mike, I can see where it began to grow when I learned to trust again. At the same time, I was in Vietnam long enough to realize that most of the grunts felt the same as I, only they felt abandoned by their country. They put their lives on the line every day, fighting what seemed to be a pointless war, while the people at home blamed them for doing their duty.

It just dawned on me, Mike and I were walking point in a pointless war. It's ironic but not funny. Mike and I had our ups and downs. There were times when I thought we were the best of buddies and I was his number one confidant. Then the stress of war would hit us, and we were at each other's throats. In the end we had to figure this out because our lives depended on each other, and so did the lives of hundreds of other soldiers.

Back in the old days when I was with mom, I was part of a pack. When I was with Dave, Sandy, and Lisa, I had a similar feeling, like I was part of a pack. When I got to Fort Benning Scout Dog School there were fifty of us canines and I was part of a pack. But with Mike I felt like I was part of a team not a pack. Every week we were with different units but not part of their pack. As a canine there is something in my soul that tells me that my destiny was to belong in a pack, and when Mike talked with me on lonely nights in the field, I thought his soul had the same longing.

I think God brought Mike and me together because we were like the Lone Ranger and Tonto. This was our opportunity to learn one-on-one how to be a member of a pack. I know that even though I fought people who got in my space, what I most wanted was someone I could trust. I wanted someone to care for me, have my back, and not abandon me. Bottom line is, I only wanted to be loved like my mom loved me. Now, as I lie here on this table reminiscing about my life, feeling abandoned, I am thinking that maybe I did achieve Superhero status.

Dog Team Down

When we arrived back at base camp, we received some tragic news. One of our dog teams was ambushed and killed in action (KIA) while on patrol. I didn't know the handler; I only saw him when he would pick up his partner, Ringo. Ringo was a pretty quiet dog as far as scout dogs go. He seemed to be well mannered and hadn't been in the country very long. Ringo and his partner hadn't been out on many patrols, so I wonder if lack of experience may have been a factor in their deaths. Fatalities were common for new recruits. It's easy to make fatal decisions when you aren't clear about all the dangers. Mike and I had three months in the field at that point, and we were just beginning to feel comfortable with our jobs. I was trusting Mike, and Mike was great at reading my alerts. We had become a first-class dog-team.

Ringo and his handler were still on the learning curve and there was a lot to learn. Like I said, Ringo seemed like a good guy. He was a few cages down from me and just out of sight. I never figured out why Dave decided to name me Chico — he never said, and I couldn't ask. Besides, it no longer matters. But I think I know how Ringo got his name. I'm fairly sure it has something to do with Beatle Mania, which was often bigger than Vietnam mania.

I know this is going to come across as shallow on my part, but during that time I was just trying to deal with my own issues. I was jealous of Ringo. There! I said it! It's not as odd as you might think. Many infantry soldiers lost friends in firefights and felt guilty that they didn't die with their buddy. I'm sure that Ringo ended up as a hometown hero along with his handler. The local papers probably told the story of his heroism, walking point in this controversial war. They probably told their readers that Ringo was a war dog decorated for meritorious action in the face of the enemy, how he bravely gave his life for the country, that he was a patriot and will live in eternal honor.

Yes, I'm jealous! Here I am, waiting to be euthanized, quietly being disposed of by the same Army that will turn Ringo's demise into a recruitment message. My heroism will be forgotten the moment the vet tech jams the needle in my front leg and pushes the plunger. Who will tell the world that I was a decorated war hero, a Superhero? I was positive that I would go down in a blaze of glory like Ringo, not on a hot metal table used to conveniently dispose of scout dogs that have served the country and saved the lives of countless soldiers. Bad-mouth me if you will, but each of us wants to leave a legacy. If I don't come back as a human, I vow to be stuck in Mike's head until the day he dies. He can tell the world what I did in this war and make sure my legacy lives on into eternity.

On another note, I'm concerned about what they did or didn't do with Ringo's body. I know the lieutenant wanted Mike to go identify the handler's body, but Mike refused to do the lieutenant's job and opted out. There was no mention of who would identify Ringo's body, and his remains didn't come back to the 46th as far as I can determine. I would guess Ringo will be an honorable mention in the handler's obituary. When is the military going to wake up and give us war dogs the respect we deserve? Ringo should have a proper military funeral and his name on a memorial wall. He died fighting for this country, for crying out loud!

The 46th was deployed to support the 25th Infantry Division. Within the 25th there was a diverse set of units, and we had already worked with several of them, mostly grunts, the backbone of Infantry. We also worked with mechanized units and worked off gun boats in the Delta, a story I'll share with you later. One of our unique assignments was on Nui Ba Den, The Black Virgin Mountain. The U.S. controlled the top of the mountain and built a fire-support base camp up there. They would helicopter a dog team in from our unit to patrol the perimeter in the evenings. I was surprised when we arrived and were briefed to find out we were going to be doing sentry dog duties inside base camp for two weeks. This duty was like being on vacation: cooler weather on top of the mountain, safer conditions inside the fire-support base camp, and decent living conditions. It wasn't uncommon to be with soldiers who were smoking dope, which provided a refuge from the crazy circumstances we experienced in this crazy war.

Well, one evening we were walking patrol around the perimeter and a few guys on bunker duty called me and Mike over to answer a few questions. It wasn't uncommon for us to get a lot of questions about what we do, but this night was a little different. One of the guys told Mike they had smoked a couple of joints and wanted to put on a light show. Confused, Mike asked him what he meant, and the guy said, "If you agree to say your dog has an alert, we can call in fire support and they will put on the light show." Mike told him we didn't care if he wanted to call in the alert because this was an odd situation.

Well, they called in an alert in my name, and ten minutes later I saw one fantastic light show, and Mike and I don't even smoke dope! Two old WWII AC-47 gunships (planes) called "Spooky" arrived with multiple mini guns firing 2000 rounds a minute straight down on the "enemy." Flares were launched from the Tay Ninh Base Camp to light up the skies to expose any VC trying to penetrate the perimeter wire. Of course, we knew this was a bogus alert for the sole purpose of high entertainment. The reality was that if I had had a real alert on top of that mountain, the wind was blowing so hard and my nose is so fantastic that I could have picked up an alert on the enemy clear back in North Dakota. Just kidding … but half serious!

Like I said, this base camp was like being on vacation, and we were up there for ten to fourteen days. Due to difficult landing conditions, the Army flew in supplies on a Chinook (large supply helicopter) on a bi-weekly schedule, and we would switch out dog teams using that flight. I should mention that it was frowned upon by most grunts for someone to smoke dope before going on patrol. We all had to cover each other's backs so being high didn't work. When we were in base camp, it was very common to have a group of handlers show up at nightfall behind our kennels and partake in passing a joint around, as they called it, usually followed by silly giggling. Silly giggling was a refreshing sound in a place where every day you woke up being thankful you hadn't gotten hit in the overnight rocket attacks, all the while wondering if it would be the day your luck ran out.

Revenge Is Sweet

As I've said, my relationship with Mike was a work in progress. There were times when I felt like I could trust him, and then there were times I felt like red flags were popping up and my abandonment issues stirred inside. This was one of those weeks when my feelings and his attitude were boiling. We were in base camp for a couple of days, and Mike and the platoon sergeant had a bad relationship. Every morning Mike would get the detail to literally burn shit. The soldiers defecated in a fifty-five-gallon drum that was cut down to about twenty-four inches. Every morning three drums had to be pulled out, fuel oil and gas added, and then set on fire to burn away the feces and toilet paper. Because of their arguments, it was a given that Mike would get that detail and that would often set Mike off. I could tell by Mike's tone when we'd run the obstacle course how angry he was with the sergeant. I usually got the yelling he couldn't give the platoon sergeant. This week something special must have occurred because Mike was on the muscle. The good news was that our orders came in and we were headed back out to the field. It was my hope Mike would chill out, because I was tired of his attitude and I was moving into the old Chico. Not pretty.

We flew into Fire Base Alpha and, as usual, Mike tied me up and headed to the command bunker to get filled in on what we were here to do. Walking away he sarcastically quipped, "Do me a favor. Don't bite any officers," and my unspoken reply was, "Tell someone who cares, I'm tired of your lip."

When Mike returned, I could tell he was wound up and he was still being short with me. Eventually he needed to vent and mentioned to me that we had a night mission to surround a village and go in at daybreak. Intel suspected that the village housed VC sympathizers, and our job was to search and destroy evidence of such activity. At that point I was in full-blown reaction to how Mike was treating me, and while I non-verbally agreed to not use biting as a revenge tool, I needed to put my thinking cap on to get my point across to Mike that we were equals.

That night they flew us out at dusk and dropped us off. We then had to patrol for a long distance, in silence, to the vicinity of the village. This is where my Superhero traits shone. My nose worked 24 hours a day, but my night sight was a big benefit in situations like that night patrol. Eventually we arrived and were deployed to surround the entire village in preparation to go in and contain the village at daybreak.

It was about three in the morning, pitch black and not a sound, except for vampire mosquitoes so large their wings hummed like a ceiling fan on high speed seeking refueling with human blood. I could tell by the way Mike was snapping my leash and tightening my choke chain that on top of a rough week in base camp, he was being eaten alive and was aggravated. Every time he'd jerk my leash, I became more committed to get even when the opportunity arose.

Around four Mike stood up and I thought we were ready to move out, but no one else moved. Then it dawned on me what was happening. Mike had to "take care of business," and in our tight quarters he just moved forward a few feet and did the dirty deed. With that, my plan fell into place.

Mike came back and sat down next to me. I decided to wait until he dozed off to make my move. Luckily, he did it within my six-foot leash distance. As much as it grossed me out, I knew this would bring my point home to him in a lasting way. He'll never forget this event. So, I commenced to roll in his fresh dump and to cover my coat as completely as possible. I must admit this was a stinking thing to do, as they say, and it killed me, but I just couldn't resist making my point.

I slowly walked back and nuzzled Mike to wake him up. He woke up, and I knew he was aggravated that I had awakened him, but he couldn't talk and give away our position. That's when I sprang the surprise: I started snuggling up to him. I could hear him gagging and trying to push me away without touching his own mess. This went on for about a half hour, and feeling I'd made my point, I laid down and left him alone.

I was proud that I had made my point but wasn't happy with the aftereffects. At daybreak he abruptly walked me to a nearby B52 bomb crater that was filled with rainwater, and he threw me in several times until I was cleaned up. A lot of the other soldiers had a field day laughing at Mike for what I did to him. The good news was that we immediately got our move-out orders to secure the village. To say the least, it had been a stressful day, and while I know I made my point, I was glad Mike never brought it up again. We seemed to just move on with our relationship.

I know I tend to focus on the negative because I find it hard to trust, but there was a lot of progress in my relationship with Mike. I hate to admit it, but I learned to love this guy. When we were on the obstacle course, we had so much fun together. It was a competition to see who could get the upper hand. I knew I had the upper paw while Mike thought he had the upper hand. When we were in the field is when it was the best. At night we were with guys we didn't know so we stayed to ourselves a lot. Mike was lonely, so he had some real deep talks with me. This is when I wished I were blessed with a human tongue. The things I would have said to Mike would comfort him I'm sure. After all, we just wanted to know we were not alone, and we had someone to love us.

I know Mike loved me because he went to bat for me often. When we were in the field and someone crossed the line and I needed to bite them, Mike was the first to defend me, telling them he had warned them to keep their distance. He never scolded me for biting once I stopped biting him. When we were in base camp some of the other handlers would bang on my cage door to get a reaction from me. I would hear Mike tell them, "Knock it off, before Chico breaks a tooth on the cage." I really appreciated him backing me up, and yes, those chain-link fences were a little tough on my teeth. But I couldn't resist responding to those handlers who thought they could push me around.

I loved the way he raked my fur backwards before brushing me. He told me what a good boy I was when he was grooming me. Man, I loved to be groomed and have him brush the stench of this place off my body. Mike was also great at rubbing behind my ears and on my belly. I was pretty good at reading Mike's moods, and when appropriate I had a way of nuzzling up to him that drew him out of his loneliness. Because we were a team, I often thought when his tour was finished and it was time for him to return to the world, I would be going with him. But it seems I was sadly mistaken.

Ambush Patrol

The next week we were out with another unit and things got a little off-track, though in the end it all worked out great. On the second day the commanding officer got some Intel that an NVA unit was headed in our direction and we needed to stop their advance. The problem was that intelligence didn't know exactly where they were. We were close to the Cambodian border and not supposed to cross into that country, so the decision was made to set up an ambush patrol in the hope of spotting and monitoring their direction. Well, lo and behold, the commanding officer decided he wanted a dog team with his unit. Mike and I were both surprised with his decision.

That evening two soldiers from the unit along with Mike and I went out to set up an ambush position. We were about two miles in front of the rest of the company and could observe a trail that was suspected of being used by the NVA. With just the four of us, we would be in deep danger if our position were to be exposed. The key to an ambush is total silence, and we were just there to observe. Each soldier was assigned to a certain timeline to be awake and observe the path through a Starlight Scope (a special night-vision binocular). Mike and I dozed off knowing he had the watch later that night. I must have been in a deep sleep because all at once something startled me and I snapped into action. The next thing I knew, I was standing on the chest of one of the soldiers we were with on patrol. Mike woke up from all the commotion and settled me down. As it turned out, the first watch had gone to wake up the second watch, and that was what startled me. That's when I pounced on the number two watch in my confused state.

The noise I made, combined with the soldiers' reactions and Mike trying to calm me down, had exposed our position, but luckily we all settled down and got quiet again. Around two in the morning, while Mike was on watch, an NVA Unit walked right down the trail a couple of hundred yards in front of us. I was on my best behavior and never made a sound, and eventually the danger passed. At dawn we headed back to join our unit and deliver the intelligence on our sighting. Later that day the Commanding Officer came and told us he had bad news. He said his men told him that Mike's dog was crazy and almost blew the operation. As a result, he put in an order to 25th Infantry Division Headquarters that we no longer would be allowed to be on ambush patrols. Talk about a stroke of good luck! Mike and I would never have to do that again. For once my aggression was in my favor!

Superhero Powers Save Lives

Decorated Superhero

On one of our assignments we were patrolling with an infantry unit and had a close call. We didn't often walk the trails because they were heavily booby-trapped. One morning we were walking a trail in thick jungle terrain, so I had to be on high alert because there was little breeze to carry the scent I needed to detect an alert on the enemy. It seemed like a typical patrol except for walking the trail, but as we turned a bend, I picked up on a faint scent and, not thinking, I gave a faint alert. I was taken aback when Mike stopped the patrol. I didn't think he had noticed my alert since it was so slight. But he called the lieutenant up and told him, "Chico gave an alert, but it's an odd one." He went on to say my alert was so faint that he thought something dangerous was awfully close. This is where my Superhero abilities came into play — nose then sight. I let Mike know, after picking up the scent and alerting, that I saw a trip wire vibrating in the sunlight about ten feet ahead. The scent was faint because the VC probably had set the trap the night before and there was little residual smell on the wire.

After Mike's warning and a brief discussion, two grunts experienced in explosives moved forward and located the trip wire. They eventually moved everyone back and detonated the explosives. I never gave it a lot of thought, and we finished out the next few days and returned to base camp. To my surprise, the next day a news crew showed up and wanted to take pictures for the *Tropic Lightning News*, a paper for the 25th Infantry Division. They gave Mike his second

Army Commendation Medal, this one with a V for Valor, and jokingly said, "We can't pin a medal on Chico, so we want you to feed him this sixteen-ounce steak so we can take his picture."

So, I got a big steak, Mike got a medal, our picture was in the news, and the story was that we were heroes for saving many lives.

If that wasn't enough, I learned later that Mike found out about Dave, my civilian owner, and wrote to him and sent him the news article. I was so excited to think that Dave, Sandy, and Lisa would know I was now a military Superhero. Months later Mike sprang a surprise on me: he opened an envelope and told me I was a hometown hero in Williston, North Dakota. Dave had given the article to a local paper and they did a story on me. You talk about proud! I hope someone thought to show the article to my mom. She wouldn't be surprised though; she knew I was special. I'd really like her to know; I love her so much! Right here is where I knew I should say, "I'm not trying to blow my own horn," but that is exactly what I want to do. Blowing my own horn is appropriate when my Superhero powers save lives!

As Superhero – I get a steak!

Monsoon

There were many challenges in Vietnam. The heat was unbearable, but I adapted like all tough grunts must, in order to survive walking patrol. And just when I got used to the heat, the monsoon season showed up. I thought I went through some pretty rough thunder and rainstorms back in North Dakota, but I was usually riding the storm out inside a warm and dry house.

I can recall so many nights in the living room with Dave and Sandy watching television and seeing reports of soldiers slogging through rice paddies with monsoon rain pouring down on them. I felt sorry for them. The conditions looked very difficult. Now that I have slogged through the same rice paddies, I can tell you the news reports didn't do justice to the experience. The rain came down so hard that it blinded us, and we often felt like we were being pelted with needles. Most of the handlers had something like jock itch on their feet, and sometimes the water was so high they got double jock itch. Dry clothes for them was not an option. I was lucky I didn't have boots and socks that allowed the water, buffalo dung, and god knows what else is stirred up by the monsoon rains to fester around my feet. Mike was rather good at looking for clean water to walk me through to clean off anything I might have picked up in the cesspools we had to patrol through.

During the monsoon season the rain came down so hard that it disrupted everything in its path. I heard Mike talk about us getting up to twenty-two inches of rain a day. It became a real challenge for me from the standpoint of it stirring up smells that had laid dormant since the end of the past monsoon season. For many reasons Vietnam had thousands of more smells than back in North Dakota. They didn't have much refrigeration and there were many open-air markets with raw meat hanging out to dry. They even had crazy stuff like monkey. On a windy day I could pick up a thousand different scents from a mile away. As a side note, one of our handler's was from the Philippines. When he was in base camp on weekends, he visited a Philippine Army Unit and guess what they like to eat? DOG! Yes, a 46th scout dog handler visited his friends, and they ate dog! What a traitor!

Sorry. I got sidetracked again, but I'm sure you can understand how I feel! Imagine for a moment you have a friend you work with and trust, and one day you find out they are a cannibal, and you go to another friend's house and they tell you they had Fred for dinner. That just might throw you for a loop, right? Now I don't know the names of the canines they ate on weekends, but if you're going to eat crazy meat, I suggest monkey, because they are about as crazy as you can get.

We, on the other hand, have gone along with your crazy human plan to domesticate us and act like we are your pets. If that isn't bad enough, you want to dress us up in silly costumes. When we were in base camp, Mike dressed me up in tee shirts, and one time in a Santa Claus hat and beard. Then he took pictures of me. I have no idea where he sent them. There I was, trying to establish myself as a Superhero, a decorated war veteran, and he was dressing me up like a clown and distributing the pictures. What if the newspaper in Williston, North Dakota, that ran the story of me being awarded a steak for alerting on a trip wire and saving the patrol, got ahold of me dressed like Santa? Sure, Mike thought it was cute. How would he have liked it if I had taken a picture of him burning human feces and sent it to his hometown paper? I'd bet he just might have been a little pissed at me. As you can see, just the thought of the monsoon rains pounding on my head causes me to go off on a crazy tangent, kind of like those crazy monkeys I used to watch on "National Geographic."

But … getting back to my story. There were times when we were on patrol that the monsoon rains held off and it looked like it was going to be a good day. We would finish our patrol still dry. That's when it always seemed to happen. On one day, we heard the choppers in the distance coming to pick us up and from the other direction we could see a wall of water headed our way. That's right, the monsoon rains literally looked like a wall. And there you have it, monsoon roulette. Which will win and arrive first, the choppers to pick us up and deliver us back to camp semi-dry, or monsoon rains to soak us to the bone?

Leeches

During the monsoon season we also got deployed down to the Delta to work off a Navy boat. The Mekong Delta was south of Tay Ninh and is the watery area of Vietnam patrolled by the Navy. When we arrived there, the Navy took our unit up-river to a designated place to be dropped off and patrol. When the boat pulled into our starting location, we were told that the water was neck deep but would recede quickly as we moved forward. Mike was hesitant but decided to join the patrol against his better judgment. It didn't look like a good idea to me either. I had never developed my swimming skills. As a matter of fact, I wasn't sure I could swim, and I heard Mike tell one of the guys that he couldn't. Oh, great!

The next thing I knew we were off the boat and in the water. Mike was up to his neck and looked a little panicked. He had all his gear on, his M16 under water, and me on his shoulder. He slowly made his way forward, but the water level remained the same. After a short time, he told me he was too tired to carry me, and he pushed me off his shoulder and made me start to swim. I felt like I could hold my own for a short while, and that's when I started to feel those little bloodsuckers hitching a ride on me. My guess was that the grunts had no clue what was happening. There was a ton of confusion because everyone was worn out, the water was still at neck level, and unannounced to everyone, transfusions had begun. Mike pulled me back up on one shoulder every so often so I wouldn't get exhausted.

Finally, the platoon leader called from the boat to tell us new orders had come in and we were to return immediately. It took us quite a while, but eventually we returned to the boat. That's when the big reveal happened. I was their first clue. I had hundreds of those slimy, beady-eyed bloodsuckers hanging off me. Suddenly the entire deck of the boat was loaded with soldiers stripping off uniforms. Everybody was covered with leeches. Talk about gross! Someone discovered that Army-issued bug repellant, when squirted on the leeches, would cause them to drop off. It was rather amusing from my perspective: fifty naked soldiers squirting bug repellant on each other, butt-checking their buddies for possible foreign invaders. It was like a day at the park with everyone checking everybody's butts. That was the first and last time we worked with the Navy, which was fine with me. I'm not a swimmer and those leeches suck, if you know what I mean?

That was when I realized more and more that I was part of a team. I knew Mike had my back, because as soon as we hit that water, even though he couldn't swim, he immediately carried me on his shoulders. Even when he was exhausted, he kept pulling me back and carrying me when he saw I was struggling. When we were back on the deck of the boat, he took the time to get all leeches off of me before tending to himself. While there is a diminished general military attitude about us war dogs in treating us like chattel, despite our rough beginning my handler treated me like I was family. I wondered what it would be like going home to Cincinnati, Ohio, with Mike and meeting the rest of the family. I know he got some delicious cookies in the mail which he always shared with me, so I wanted to meet the great chef. I know now it will never happen.

Every now and then I got to take a tour of Mike's barracks when we were in base camp. There were 10 or 12 rooms in each barrack, and his room was in the middle. I liked it when he invited me into his space. It let me know he cared for me. His room was small, not much larger than my accommodations, but he had a bed to lie on instead of a concrete floor. He had pictures of movie stars with their teats exposed. If I could talk, I would have told Mike to write Dave and request a picture of my mom on her back with all her teats on display. I could have hung that picture of mom in my kennel for nights when I felt lonely. I think she would have been honored. She would have been proud to know she nursed a Superhero who saved lives in the Vietnam War.

As a canine it was easy to see prejudice and how it affected the way we were treated differently from our handlers. When I walked through the barracks, I noticed it was set up much like our kennel. Rooms were on each side to house the soldiers, with a main aisle down the center with an exit on each end. Each housing cubical had a bed and an open doorway for soldiers to enter and exit at will. They could enter each room if they wanted to visit and chat with fellow soldiers. Like our accommodations, you could see these were lacking both in comfort and freedom of movement.

If it really mattered to the top brass, they could have made some changes. They could have provided a bed, with four concrete blocks to keep the bed safe from pee, poop, and clean-up. A metal frame with springs for flex, and a dog mattress. Voila! And how about a little socializing? The Army could add some time at Scout Dog School, to socialize all of us to coexist once we reach our assigned duty. How about leaving the individual kennel doors open so we could hang out with our own and socialize as we desire? The Army could keep the main kennel doors secured to deter any thoughts by canine radicals to slip out back and smoke a joint together. (I know, I just can't resist sarcasm!)

I often use sarcasm to relay a deeper message. The military didn't do a very good job of helping the grunts deal with the stresses of war, so the grunts took it upon themselves to try to comfort and calm themselves down, usually by drinking too much or smoking dope. I'm not here to cast aspersions on any of the handlers, because they too were in a tough position walking point every day. From my perspective the military never even considered what us scout dogs went through, and what might help us take care of our mental health. I mean, after all, the military can't claim ignorance when it comes to the effect humans have on dog behavior. Just look at the bum rap that Pit Bulls and Doberman breeds have gotten over the years. Humans train these dogs to be aggressive, and then other humans condemn the dogs' behavior after they have been trained by humans. I hope one day someone will step up and honor the American War Dogs with the respect and honor they deserve. I'm speaking for all of us — scout, sentry, tracker, tunnel, and any other venue in which we save lives and make a difference.

Well, I know I've been on my soap box preaching away. Life is just full of irony. One example I haven't shared is that the handlers could take a shower when we returned from the field to wash off the week, albeit a primitive shower. Once every few months I got to go to the dip tank. Mike would escort me to a concrete tank filled with water and some chemical to ward off fleas, ticks, and other war-like varmints. The technique used was rather awkward. He put his arms around my four legs, lifted me up and flipped me head-first into the tank. This was done to ensure my entire body got submerged in the solution, ears, and all, followed by me exiting as fast as possible, followed by rounds of shaking. The stuff smelled bad, so I wouldn't classify it as a shower. It was more like a mud puddle bath if you get my gist.

Mike flipped me headfirst into the dip tank.

Thoroughly soaked I was ready for bug free living.

With a little help from Mike, I made a quick exit.

Hornets

One thing the magical dip didn't deter was hornets. The reason I know is, while on a patrol I accidentally disturbed a hornet's nest in the ground. The way those hornets swarmed and attacked you would have thought they were killer bees like I'd heard about from Dave and was concerned they would become part of my responsibility in protecting Lisa from those devil critters. And if you've ever snatched a wasp from the air with your mouth, you know the pain you can experience. It was a skill set I decided not to hone!

The hornet attack happened in a matter of seconds. I was being stung and yelping at the top of my lungs. Mike was trying to knock them off me, but quickly he was being attacked too. He took off running and pulled me along to get out of the area. I know I tend to exaggerate, but we both were literally covered with hornet stings to the point where we were pulled off-line for a few days to take care of our wounds. I'll never forget the day this happened: July 20, 1969. The reason I remember the date is when we got settled in, someone came into our bunker and announced that Neil Armstrong had just landed on the moon. Once again, we had a hot story: headline — Superhero War Dog Attacked by Killer Hornets! But no, I got upstaged by a "moon walk." It's the story of my life. Seriously, the hornet stings were bad enough that we were given shots and medication to help the swelling go down.

The other thing the magical dip didn't seem to stop was mosquitoes. Vietnam was the perfect breeding ground for "ninja mosquitoes." These suckers (pun intended) are so big that I think they could draw a pint of blood with one stick in the body. One of the handlers referred to them as Vietnam's national bird. I was surprised the military hadn't recruited and trained them to draw blood or perform transfusions. After all, they used us canines for their benefit, so why not take advantage of the bumper crop of those ruthless mosquitoes? When we slogged through the rice paddies, they flew out by the hundreds. At dusk, it was like someone declared open season on infantry soldiers out in the field. Back in base camp, some of the handlers had mosquito nets over their beds so they could sleep soundly without the bloodsuckers driving them crazy.

Vietnam seemed to be a land of aggravating critters. The blood-sucking mosquitoes had another partner in crime. The Vietnamese people used water buffalos to carry their crops and plow their fields. When you put a water buffalo in a rice paddy, you can bet it is going to stir up a swarm of mosquitoes looking to suck some American soldier's blood. These ugly animals were so important to the farmers that they were kept in the huts at night, just like family.

I once saw an interesting water buffalo special on "National Geographic." People have been working with them for over five thousand years. That's when they were domesticated, you know, to serve the master race! In the wild they can grow to seven feet tall and weigh twenty-five hundred pounds. That's a lot of big and ugly! After domestication they were bred to be smaller, six-hundred and fifty to twelve-hundred pounds, but still excessively big animals and still ugly. Like I said, they were used to plow for planting crops, and to carry crops during the harvest. They were also used for survival.

They provided meat and milk, and their horns and hides were sold or made into useful items. A few special facts especially got my attention. Their milk is used to make the best mozzarella cheese. So, the next time you order a large Italian pizza, ask them for extra water buffalo and see what they say! And just guess what kind of noise they make? A quacking noise! Did you know dinosaurs are also thought to have quacked? In Vietnam, the way their hair grows on their pelt can mean good luck. If the hair grows evenly, creating a symmetrical pattern, it means the owner will have good luck and good health. In other words, the Vietnamese received all the benefits, and we got all the mosquitoes they stirred up. The water buffalo is the Vietnamese national animal and the American pain in the ass! The reality of war is often the back story and I have experienced many versions of back stories in Vietnam!

When I used to watch the news reporters, I thought I was getting the full story of the Vietnam conflict, "the living room war," as they called it. But having been here, I realized it seemed like I was getting a political dissertation on the war, along with the carnage. What I wasn't getting was the everyday struggle the grunts and I worked with in our quest to stay alive. That's really what the war came down to. We were all just trying to stay alive, hoping to go home at the end of our tours, to go back to "The World" and see our friends and families.

You can't believe how many nights I longed to be back home with Lisa, letting her drive me crazy with that blue squeaky toy. I dreamed of lying on my mom's chest one more time, feeling her nose nuzzling up to my ear, back when life was simple and safe. But I knew in my heart of hearts my chances of getting out of this hellhole war were slim to none. My epitaph will be,

"Left Behind — Nobody Cares!" Let the leeches suck the blood out of my body and the mosquitoes carry me away to my final resting place — probably a rice paddy!

Peanut Butter

I had my ways of messing with Mike, and he had his ways of messing with me. One of his favorite things to do was feed me peanut butter. When we were in the field the troops often had to eat C-rations, horrible military food in a can. Mike especially hated this one meal, ham, and lima beans. He would gag if he tried to eat it. Many times, he'd just skip the meal and throw it away, but in the box with the meal there was a small tin of peanut butter and a packet of crackers. Mike would keep those to feed to me. He knew I absolutely loved peanut butter and I couldn't resist eating it whenever it was available. This wasn't something he did because he loved me. He had an ulterior motive. He would usually have a few guys with him and then he would tell his audience what to look for when he fed me. He would usually say, "You're going to love this. When I hold the can of peanut butter out for Chico to lick, watch the way he moves his tongue when the peanut butter starts to stick to the roof of his mouth." They would all laugh hysterically while watching me try to get globs of sticky peanut butter off the roof of my mouth. It was worth the humiliation though. I got to eat my favorite food, and I got to cheer up Mike and the troops. I was like a mini USO show. Once again, my tongue is useless beyond lapping water and licking my butt. The military removed my balls, so one less thing to lick. If there is a dog heaven, I bet everything is coated with peanut butter.

Abandoned Again

The Dreaded Ending

Our year together went much faster than I would have imagined. We had some of the most dangerous days of our collective lives. We got to see Vietnam from every angle, flying in three different types of choppers, high above the jungles and rice paddies; riding tanks and APC's down mine-laden roads and through rubber-tree plantations; working off of boats in the Mekong Delta region; chopping through dense jungle; navigating B-52 bomb craters; and trying to avoid the areas freshly sprayed with Agent Orange used to de-foliate the land. You name it, we patrolled in it. We saved lives and had several close calls, but we made it while walking point, one of the most dangerous jobs to have on a patrol.

One magic day it happened. Mike's prediction came true. They told Mike he was being taken off-line. We had been sent out in the field more often than the others because of Mike's run-in with the platoon sergeant when we first arrived at the 46th. I remember Mike had predicted if we didn't get killed, we would be pulled off-line earlier, and he was right. We still had about a month until he went back to "The World." Now he just had to avoid getting hit by one of the many rockets that the VC would fire into our base camp every night starting around dinner time.

I wasn't clear what my status was. Mike continued to exercise me, and we had much more time to talk. He told me they made him Supply Sergeant, which was basically a non-position with a title. He was a sergeant before coming off-line — that was true, but there were no supplies to speak of, other than a jeep and our gear. But the rebel I came to love was still alive in Mike. Now that he was an off-line sergeant, he blew their minds as he continued to burn feces every morning, as if nothing had changed. Since he had rank, he could have delegated the job to one of the new guys, but for some reason, he didn't. I think it was his way of saying, "You can't get to me!" That was the very thing that made us a perfect team. Both of us loners with a chip on our shoulders — never to be broken! Now we had more time to hang out and just talk, but I didn't like what I heard. He told me that he would be heading home real soon and that made me sad. Then he started talking about me getting a new handler. And that made me angry!

The thought of breaking in a new handler wasn't something I looked forward to. I had put way too much time and energy into my relationship with Mike and finally learned to trust him. I didn't want to start all over again. Why in the hell couldn't I ship out with Mike? We were a team and we belonged with each other. I was not sure I could handle the disappointment. I loved this guy and I wanted to live out the rest of my days by his side. I knew he felt the same way about me. He got choked up whenever he talked about leaving. I could see the conflicted look on his face and smell the anger on him whenever he thought about leaving me behind.

The next few weeks flew by and then one day Mike entered my kennel, took a knee, put his arms around me, and said, "I love you, boy! I'm sorry there is nothing I can do about this. I'm sorry. I love you, boy! Take care of yourself. Goodbye, Chico. Thanks for saving my life! I promise I will never forget what a hero you are in my eyes." Then I heard a voice say, "Time to go, Monahan. Jeep's waiting."

And just like that it was over. Once again, I was all alone — abandoned.

Abandoned again.

My Tour Continues

I had a few weeks to sit in my kennel and digest what had just happened. I hated to act like a victim, but this theme seems to be a reoccurring nightmare in my life. How did this happen to me? What am I doing here, left behind in a foreign country? Why am I not in charge of my own life? Why is it that my reward for doing a stellar job always seems to turn out to be abandonment? I'm done! I quit! Mike is gone and I am just tattoo number 66A9.

The Superhero had exited my body. I'm just a stupid, old, mean dog once more. A new handler showed up and I went through the same old routines and did what was expected from me. I bit him and fought every command he gave me. We patrolled and I did my job. I was a scout dog and I was committed to saving lives. I got him through his tour of duty safely too. But I had made two vows when Mike said good-bye. I vowed that Mike was the last guy I would trust with my heart. From that moment on, I was just military equipment — expendable. That was the way the military saw us war dogs. The other vow I made was to tag on to something Mike told me right before leaving, "I promise I will never forget what a hero you are in my eyes." At that moment, I used my Superhero powers to put a magical spell on him: "You will tell the world about me and declare my heroism until the day you die!" And with that, I bestowed a long life on him, filled with triumphs, disasters, successes, and failures, so he could draw on the lessons we learned together walking point!

Hot Metal Table

After the last handler finished his tour of duty, the decision was made by higher ups to go ahead and put me down. Even though I still had it in me to scout, the brass didn't want to mess around with my aggressive approach to making sure my handlers had the right stuff. I haven't lived very long, but I sure have had the opportunity to experience some of life's greatest challenges. If I ever come back as a human, I would surely make a great relationship therapist. I could help others express their feelings and master the art of communication to produce better relationships. If I didn't do that, I would probably be an Army "lifer," making sure I was positioned to make significant changes in how war dogs are treated. But I think that's a long shot, so I'll go to the Great Beyond, believing Mike, my handler and friend, will one day profess to the world my Superhero status and what a difference I made while we were together, inspiring others to help every dog in need of love.

I think it's time for me to join the Big Dog Pack in the sky. I just heard the front door open and can hear the vet tech rustling through his utensils. I can't believe it — his assistant just put a muzzle on me! Boy, how quickly people can jump on the bandwagon when someone starts a rumor like, "Chico is crazy, we need to put him down! Too Aggressive!" Sure, take away the little dignity I have left after a two-year tour in Vietnam. A hot metal table, no friends to say goodbye, and muzzled as I'm about to be put down.

I decided it was my last opportunity to take charge and still be the Superhero. In my mind I ran a movie of my life. I could feel myself lying on my mom's chest with her nose nuzzling in my ear. Dave, Lisa, Sandy, and Lois appeared, and took turns holding me and telling me how much they loved me. And just like that, Mike walked up with a scouting harness. "Come on, boy. It's time to do your thing!" Mike put my scouting harness on me, hooked a leash up, and gave the command, "Scout!"

As I took point and began to move forward, my mom by my side, Mike, Lois, Dave, Sandy, and Lisa behind, I realized I had my own pack and was loved. I felt a sudden prick in my front leg, and I felt the warmth of love cover my body. Finally, I know I am Chico, Superhero Extraordinaire, at peace with life, as I complete my final patrol.

Epilogue

Life has a unique way of working to line up events that lead to becoming a Superhero. Chico could have spent his entire life being the pet of David Stuen, but Chico knew he was destined for greatness. Dave could have been selfish but instead donated Chico to the military to serve a greater purpose. Had Chico not defended Lisa from the meterman and Dave not donated Chico to the Army, I might have died in Vietnam along with many others.

Chico made a great impression on me when I was 20 years old, and here I am some 50 years later feeling a sense of responsibility to give him a voice. I have written and published five books. My first book, *From the Jungle to the Boardroom*, was released in 2011 and consisted of leadership stories about my tour in Vietnam with Chico.

While many feelings remain unsettled in me from the war, this book is my attempt to settle the feeling that bothers me most. Chico saved my life and the lives of others, and like all the dog handlers, I had to leave my partner behind. It didn't sit well with me then or now. Early records aren't clear, but over 4,245 dogs were sent to Vietnam, and most of them were left behind. At the time the military viewed dogs as equipment. It is estimated those very dogs saved well over 10,000 lives.

Chico wasn't equipment. He was my partner. He had my back. But in the end, I couldn't cover his. This book is a story of abandonment in the voice of Chico, as I imagine he might have felt, not having a voice to tell his story.

The U.S. military has changed. It now treats War Dogs as the heroes they are, with proper honors and burials. I am happy the change has happened for our four-legged soldiers.

My Superpower put a lifetime spell on Mike.

Chico's Scrapbook

CHICO · 66A9

SUPERHERO

Page Eight, THE HERALD, Williston, N.D., Thursday, Dec. 4, 1969

Former Willistonite
Becomes War Hero

A Williston war veteran, revered by his GI friends in combat, received no Bronze Star for alerting his unit to two booby traps, several enemy bunkers and numerous fresh enemy trails while on a recent patrol.

Instead, he received a thick, juicy steak — raw.

Chico, now about three and one-half years old, is a German Shepherd dog who used to belong to the Dave Stuen family. But about a year ago, Stuen, Williston policeman, and his family bid goodby to their beloved pet who just wasn't suited for "town life" and sent him on his way to Lackland Air Force Base in Texas for training in the Canine Corps.

He eventually wound up in South Vietnam with the 46th Scout Dog Platoon, distinguishing himself in combat and endearing himself in particular to Charlie Company, 4th Battalion (Mechanized), 23rd Infantry Tomahawks.

Usefulness of the 23 dogs in the 46th Scout Dog platoon has been proven time and time again. Trained to detect booby traps, punji pits and enemy personnel, they have been worth their weight in Bronze Stars on many occasions.

Platoon commander, First Lt. Richard A. Hale of Lakewood, Calif., said, "They're just as big an asset to a day patrol as a starlight scope is to a night patrol." He said the dogs can smell 40 times better than humans, hear 20 times better and see 10 times better.

In one recent month, the 46th's dogs detected 21 AK-47 rifles, 19 RPG rounds, 34 Chicom grenades, 16 mortar rounds, four bangalore torpedos, 600 rounds of small arms ammunition and one anti-tank gun.

In addition, the faithful canines uncovered many rocket rounds, Communist equipment stockpiles and hundreds of enemy bunkers. And they also provided an early warning system for numerous would-be enemy ambushes and for dozens of Red snipers.

CHICO IS SHOWN with his master, Dave Stuen, Williston police officer, about a year ago just before being shipped to an air base in Texas where he underwent training preparatory to service with the 46th Scout Dog Platoon in Vietnam.   (Herald Photo)

Chico's handler is Specialist 4 Mike Monahan of Cincinnati, Ohio. It was he who rewarded Chico with his delectable raw steak. Much better than a Bronze Star he wouldn't welcome pinned to his fur and a citation he couldn't read anyway.

When I became a home-town Superhero.

Going Off To War

Williston Police Officer Dave Stuen, shown here with his three and a half-year-old daughter, Lisa, is sending his German Shepherd, 'Chico,' off to serve with Uncle Sam. The two and a half-year-old male animal will soon be on his way to Lackland Air Force Base, Tex., where he will be trained as a guard dog for use with the Air Force. Although the Stuen family has had 'Chico' since he was a puppy, they reluctantly reached the decision that he wasn't a 'town dog.' 'Chico' will follow in the footsteps of several Williston area dogs now with the military forces.

(Herald Photo)

Saying goodbye to my family.

Certificate of Vaccination

I certify that I have this date vaccinated the animal(s) described below:

Name _Chico_

Breed _Mixed_

Number _23358_ Age _SMO_

Markings _BLK/BROWN_

Sex _M_ Weight _80#_

Vac. Against _RABIES_

Product _CEO_

Product _FROMM_

Remarks ___

Owner _DAVID_ Address _TIOGA, N.D_

Date _3 JUNE 67_ Veterinarian _R.E. Hubbard DVM_

The vet certified me ready for service.

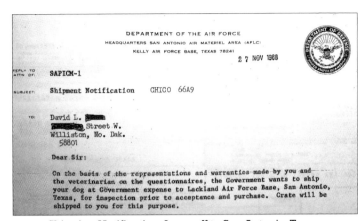

DEPARTMENT OF THE AIR FORCE
HEADQUARTERS SAN ANTONIO AIR MATERIEL AREA (AFLC)
KELLY AIR FORCE BASE, TEXAS 78241

2 7 NOV 1968

REPLY TO
ATTN OF: SAPICM-1

SUBJECT: Shipment Notification   CHICO 66A9

TO: David L. ▮▮▮▮
           ▮▮▮▮▮ Street W.
           Williston, No. Dak.
           58801

Dear Sir:

On the basis of the representations and warranties made by you and
the veterinarian on the questionnaires, the Government wants to ship
your dog at Government expense to Lackland Air Force Base, San Antonio,
Texas, for inspection prior to acceptance and purchase. Crate will be
shipped to you for this purpose.

Shipping Notification. I was off to San Antonio, Texas.

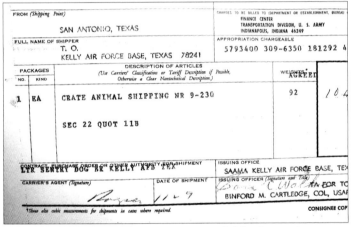

The Army even sent me a personal shipping crate.

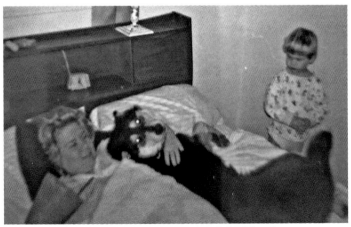

With Sandy and Lisa – my original family.

Snuggled up watching TV with Sandy.

My favorite pastime was watching the news.

Posing with Mike in Vietnam.

Mike loved to have his picture taken with a Superhero like me.

Mike dressed me up as Santa for Christmas.

Another silly costume – one cool looking dog!

My home at the 46th Scout Dog Platoon.

Some of my friends at the 46th.

Acknowledgements

Acknowledgements

I would like to thank Ken Williamson, author of *"Saying Goodbye to Vietnam,"* for our many years of friendship and convincing me to return to Vietnam in 2005, and for his support in every aspect of the journey to bring this book to life.

Thank you also to Thane Maynard, Director of the Cincinnati Zoo & Botanical Garden, an author of over a dozen books and the host of NPR's "The 90-Second Naturalist." Thane is a friend and has been an inspiration and example of the importance of protecting animals. Thanks for supporting my effort to keep Chico's promise alive through helping dog rescues and sharing his Superhero story.

Thanks to all my supporters and followers who have read my previous five books, attended my seminars, listened to my speeches, embraced my coaching, and encouraged me to continue to go for my dreams.

Thanks to Sarah Skinner for the first edit to help me get started on this project.

Thanks to Mary Fahnestock-Thomas for helping to make this the best book possible by doing the final edit.

Many thanks to Alicia Riley for the Chico artwork, you captured the spirit of Chico.

Thanks to David Stuen, his wife Sandy, daughter Lisa, and his sister Lois for donating Chico to the U.S. Army and for 50 years of support.

Thanks to my wife Nancy, my five adult children and their

spouses, and my five grandchildren, for your love and support. I would also like to thank my former wife, Mary, the mother of our four children.

My biggest thank you goes to Chico. Without you saving my life, none of the above would have happened.

The Stuen Family: Lois, David, Sandy, and Lisa

About the Author

Mike Monahan is a native of Cincinnati, Ohio and served in the United States Army as a Scout Dog Handler for the 46th Scout Dog Platoon in Tay Ninh, Vietnam from May of 1969 until April 1970. His partner's name was Chico, Military Tattoo #66A9. Mike earned the rank of Sergeant E5 and was awarded the Bronze Star, two Army Commendation Medals, one with V (Valor) and an Air Medal. Following Vietnam, he spent 22 years in construction followed by 19 years as executive director of a personal growth seminar company and lead facilitator of personal growth seminars for 16 years. As an accomplished author, Mike has written and published 5 additional books.

Monahan Family

Mike, Doogie and Nancy Monahan

Courtney and Holly Mueller,
and Brad Monahan

Coleen, Zach, and Justin Wiener

Brian, Ella, and Megan Monahan

Anne and Russ Eckert

Back: Rob, Julie, and Emma Hogan
Front: Mary Monahan, Corinn and Michael Hogan

Kickstarter Donors

Bassett, Linda

Bauke, Julie

Berning, Steve

Bol, Jan Willem

Bray, Joe

Brooks, Julie

Buck, Rain & Corey

Burroughs, Krystal

Bush, Kim

Bushman, Tracy

Cain, Brett

Cones, Marilyn

The Crawford Family

Daniher, Angela

Day, Mary

Dodge, Phillip

Dorsey, Jeff

Douglas, Betty & Jim

Eckert, Anne & Russ

Egnor, Mary

Eisenhart, Mary

Epstein, Daniel

Fitzgerald, Cindy & Ray

Fowler, Michelle

Froehle, Maria

Frye, Kevin

Garner, Bill

Garvey, Regina

Gibbons, Doris

Griffith, Karen

Groob, Jeffrey

Hamilton, Cheryl

Hayhurst, Marge & Everett

Helmer, Terry

Hoeweler, Alan & Arleen

Hogan, Julie & Rob

Hogan, Corinn & Emma

Hogan, Michael

Holtkamp, Dave

Howard, Arlene & Seth

Hudson, June & Phil

Jansen, Mary Jo & Dan

Kay, Debbie Dietrich

Kehoe, Steve

Keller, Thomas

Kelly, Matthew

Kelm, Amy

Koester, Terri & Willie

Kohnen, Madonna

Krause, Paul

LaClair, Karin

Lanier, Pat

Lesiak, Paul

Lewis, Laurie & Andy

Livingston, Ann

Marx, Kathy & Mitch

Masters, Shawn W.

Mathile, Peg

Maull, Charlie

Maxwell, Natalie

Mayer, Joe

Maynard, Thane

McKee, Craig

Metheney, Leslie

Meyer, Robin

Monahan, Brad

Monahan, Megan & Brian

Monahan, Ella

Monahan, Diane

Monahan, Jay

Monahan, Doogie & Nancy

Monahan, Thom

Moorman, Anne

Mueller, Courtney & Holly

Murphree, Amanda

Nead, Helen & Denny

Nolan, Sheila

Opanasets, Karen

Park Hills Animal Hospital

Stuen Patton, Lisa

Pennington, Dana

Pennington, Michele

Peters, Greg

Plettner, Deb & Jim

Potts, Ken

Premier Global Transportation

Ragsdale, Kaitlyn

Redman, Ben

Reed, Mike

Reilly, Vicki

Riley, Alicia & Donny

Ritchie Voegtly, Susan

Robb, Lou Ann

Rodgers, Cynthia

Rolfes, Carolyn

Rolfes, Gail & Dan

Rosato, Mary Beth

Russo, Stephanie

Ryker, Christie

Saultz, Ariel & English
   Bulldog Feisty

Schardt, Nicky & Steve

Schuster, Dianna & Randy

Sheckman, Julie

Silcott, Donny

Skinner, Sarah

Small, John

Spiker, Suzanne

Stephens, Doug

Stephens, Jim

Stetter, Pat & Bill

Stuen, Sandy & David

Sweeney, Jim

Tanis, Peg & Steve

Fahnestock-Thomas, Mary

Thomas, Tim

Tobias, John

Toft, Ken

Uhrina, Katie & Tony

Vetter, Linda & William

Waechter, Timothy

Wallace, Patricia

Walls, Megan

Weber, Ann & Mike Mitzel

Wiener, Coleen & Justin

Wiener, Zach

Wilder, Sarah & Sam

Williamson, Ken

Wilson, Lori

Wynn, Tammy

Zimmer, Melissa

South Vietnam
Military Map 1969

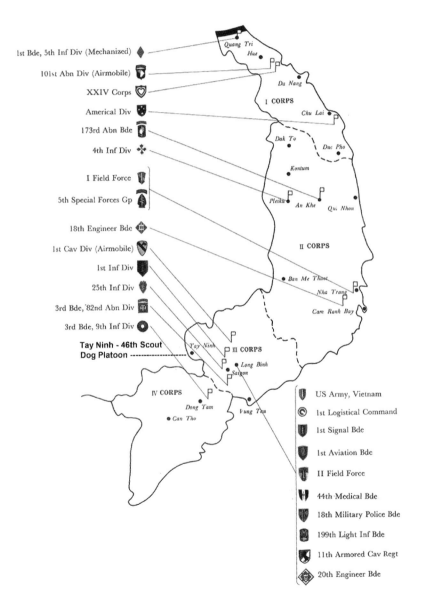

1st Bde, 5th Inf Div (Mechanized)

101st Abn Div (Airmobile)

XXIV Corps

American Div

173rd Abn Bde

4th Inf Div

I Field Force

5th Special Forces Gp

18th Engineer Bde

1st Cav Div (Airmobile)

1st Inf Div

25th Inf Div

3rd Bde, 82nd Abn Div

3rd Bde, 9th Inf Div

Tay Ninh - 46th Scout Dog Platoon - - - - - - - -

Quang Tri

Hue

Da Nang

I CORPS

Chu Lai

Dak To

Duc Pho

Kontum

Pleiku   An Khe   Qui Nhon

II CORPS

Ban Me Thuot

Nha Trang

Cam Ranh Bay

Tay Ninh   III CORPS

Long Binh

Saigon

IV CORPS

Dong Tam

Can Tho

Vung Tau

US Army, Vietnam

1st Logistical Command

1st Signal Bde

1st Aviation Bde

II Field Force

44th Medical Bde

18th Military Police Bde

199th Light Inf Bde

11th Armored Cav Regt

20th Engineer Bde